SPIRIT
AND
RESISTANCE

SPIRIT

AND

RESISTANCE

Political Theology and American Indian Liberation

George E. "Tink" Tinker

Fortress Press / Minneapolis

SPIRIT AND RESISTANCE
Political Theology and American Indian Liberation

Scripture quotations are the author's own unless otherwise noted. Those from the New
Revised Standard Version Bible, copyright © 1989 by the Division of Christian Education of
the National Council of the Churches of Christ in the USA, are used by permission.

The poem on pages 1–2, "Starting at the Bottom," is from *Woven Stone* by Simon J. Ortiz
(Tucson: University of Arizona Press, 1992). Used by permission of the author.

Cover design: Brad Norr
Author photo: Loring Abeyta
Interior design: Zan Ceeley

Library of Congress Cataloging-in-Publication Data
Tinker, George E.
Spirit and resistance : political theology and American Indian liberation / George E. "Tink"
Tinker.
  p. cm.
 Includes bibliographical references and index.
 ISBN 0-8006-3681-3 (pbk : alk. paper)
  1. Indians of North America—Religion. 2. Indians of North America—Ethnic identity.
3. Indians of North America—Government relations. 4. Liberation theology—North Amer-
ica. 5. Christianity and other religions—North America. 6. Christianity and culture—North
America. 7. Racism—Religious aspects—Christianity. 8. Civil rights—Religious aspects—
Christianity. 9. Religion and politics—North America. I. Title.
 E98.R3T56 2004
 973.04'97—dc22
                                                      2004011401

The paper used in this publication meets the minimum requirements of American National
Standard for Information Sciences—Permanence of Paper for Printed Library Materials,
ANSI Z329.48-1984.

Manufactured in the U.S.A.
08   07   06   05   04   1   2   3   4   5   6   7   8   9   10

To my father,

GEORGE EDWARD TINKER III,

and all his Osage ancestors,

and to my mother,

CAROL WICKS TINKER,

and her Lutheran Norwegian ancestors.

They have nurtured all that is good in who I am.

Contents

Preface

In the Spirit of Big Soldier:
Defending American Indian Cultures and Religious Values

In 1803 the United States purchased the entirety of Osage land—from France. Osages yet today are trying to figure that one out. It had to do with something called the Louisiana Purchase and something having to do with some obscure european legal doctrine called the "right of discovery." What it ever had to do with the Osage people, who were never privy to this doctrine or included in the negotiation leading to the purchase, is still a mystery. It was nevertheless a powerful intellectual idea, mere words in a sense, that enabled Mr. Jefferson to double the size of his country overnight.

In 1822, less than two decades later, an Osage named *a-ki'-da ton-ka*,[1] or Big Soldier as it was translated into english, returned from an official Osage delegation visiting Washington, D.C. Big Soldier's response to Washington's official wooing and his resistance to the colonizing pressure of the White world was typical of many Indian people. His words, however, have been preserved by an Indian agent for posterity as a classic voicing of Indian resistance. Deloria calls this response "the best thing any Indian ever said":

> I see and admire your manner of living, your good warm houses, your extensive corn-fields, your gardens, your cows, oxen, work-horses, wagons and a thousand machines that I know not the use of; I see that you are able to clothe yourselves, even from weeds and grass. In short, you can do almost what you choose. You whites possess the power of [subduing] almost every animal [to your] use. You are surrounded by slaves. Everything about you is in

chains, and you are slaves yourselves. I fear if I should exchange
my pursuits for yours, I too should become a slave. Talk to my
sons; perhaps they may be persuaded to adopt your fashions, or at
least to recommend them to their sons; but for myself, I was born
free, was raised free, and wish to die free. . . . I am perfectly con-
tented with my condition.[2]

Having seen the center of euro-american power, having seen the great city
of Washington, Big Soldier came away singularly unimpressed. Osages had
already experienced the technological edge—especially in military prowess—
that euro-americans had developed. And Big Soldier to some degree pays homage to the economic power of the White world, even as he rejects its apparent
benefits in favor of his own world and its sense of balance and freedom.

But even the memory of this event is clouded by euro-american mythmak-
ing that moves subtly toward discrediting Osage notions of resistance, harmony, and freedom. The problem here is that Big Soldier's name does not
really translate as Big Soldier. The translation actually presumes the White,
euro-western stereotype of Indian peoples—namely, that Indians were militaristic societies where all the men were "warriors" or "braves." It perpetuates
the euro-american myth that Indian men customarily and recklessly pursued
some warrior ideal, living in militaristic societies that gave in to primitive
blood thirst with constant warfare. Yet there is really no word for "soldier" or
even "warrior" in Osage, a lack that is consistent with all precontact Indian
communities in North America.

Thus, *a-ki'-da ton-ka*, or big *a-ki'-da*, is really a problematic name to translate into english. While some want to translate *a-ki'-da* as "warrior," and the
word was used to name the members of a military detachment, there is, as I
just said, no word for warrior or soldier in Osage or any other Indian language.
Indian war making was relatively nonviolent prior to european contact and
ultimately oriented toward the defense of the people.[3] The total destruction or
conquest of an enemy was never a military objective. Indeed, the killing of an
enemy was not usually accorded the same high honor as "counting coup," or
touching an enemy in battle without being touched in return.

A-ki'-da really refers to defense, that is, defense of the village or defender of
the people. A big *a-ki'-da* would undoubtedly be one of the five *a-ki'-da*
appointed by each of the two *ga-hi'-ga* (chiefs?), who then would have special
responsibilities for maintaining order in the town and would have lived immediately around the chiefs' houses in the center of the village. Thus, they served
a political function in each town.[4] Another example of *a-ki'-da* are the *mon-sho$^{n'}$*
a-ki-da, or those who "watch over the land."[5] These were members of a society

whose task was the defensive patrol of Osage heartlands. A couple members of the society were always on patrol to monitor enemy incursions into Osage land and to give Osage towns adequate notice for protecting themselves.

This volume is written in the spirit of Big Soldier, in the spirit of the Osage concept of *a-ki'-da*. It is presented as an act of defense and resistance to the continuing colonization of Indian peoples in North America. Thus, it speaks to a broad range of topics from the globalization of capital to the complexities of contemporary Indian identity. In particular, it presents a beginning point for voicing an American Indian theology of liberation. It was his love of freedom that caused Big Soldier to reject the appeal for him to adopt euro-american ways. As Burns argues, Big Soldier could readily appreciate the material culture of americans but resolutely rejected their spiritual culture.[6]

A preface would be incomplete without remembering those who have helped make this book a reality. Special thanks to the following persons from the American Indian and other indigenous communities for their encouragement, advice, editorial assistance, corrections, insights, and challenges. Many of these friends and relatives have read the manuscript or parts of it and have criticized it freely and constructively. My Osage relatives Morris Lookout (deceased) and Larry Sellers come first to mind. There have been numerous American Indian colleagues, the most significant of whom include Professor Glenn Morris, Professor Richard Grounds, Professor Ward Churchill, Josh Dillebaugh, Annerika Whitebird, Brett Shelton, Don Ragona, Marlene Rouillard, Anne Marshall, the Rev. Kenneth Deere, and Tony Beltham. And numerous indigenous voices from around the world have helped me in various ways to shape myself intellectually as an indigenous person. Edward and Gladys Antonio (both are Shona from southern Africa; he is my professorial colleague at Iliff School of Theology), Pastor Antonio Otzoy and Maria Juvila-juj (both Cachiqueles), Hermandad de los Presbiterios Mayas in Guatemala, and Pastor Hector Castañeda Juarez (Maya mestizo), also in Guatemala. My doctoral student Eric Larsen put countless hours into reading and editing the manuscript. The final version is immeasurably better for his generous reading and criticism. Dr. Loring Abeyta is a Chicana reader of the text and my wife. Like Eric, she has left an indelible mark on the finished text.

A Note about Word Usage

In the following chapters, my use of the lowercase for adjectives such as *english, christian, protestant, catholic, european,* and *american* is intentional. While the noun might be capitalized out of respect for each christian—as for each Muslim or Buddhist—using the lowercase *christian* or *biblical* allows us to avoid any unnecessary normativizing or universalizing of the principal institutional religious quotient of the Euro-west. The language of "christian civilization" was widely used during the conquest. It is an explicit part of Bishop Henry Benjamin Whipple's programmatic missionizing on the north-central plains in the latter half of the nineteenth century. See my analysis of Whipple in chapter 5 of *Missionary Conquest: The Gospel and Native American Genocide* (Minneapolis: Fortress Press, 1993). Paradoxically, I insist on capitalizing the *W* in *White* (adjective or noun) to indicate a clear cultural pattern invested in Whiteness that is all too often overlooked or even denied by american Whites.

1

Liberation and Sustainability
Prolegomenon to an American Indian Theology

The truth is,
most of us didn't know
much about the unions
at any rate.
A job was a job.
You were lucky to have one
if you got one.
The truth is,
the companies didn't much care
nor did the unions,
even if both of them
were working our land.

When the mines came
to the Laguna and Acoma land,
the men and their families were glad
in a way because
the men wouldn't have to go
so far away to work
for the railroad in Barstow,
Richmond, Flagstaff, Needles.
Or to pick beets and onions
in Idaho, Utah, and Colorado.
Or work for the Mormons

in Bluewater Valley
who paid you in carrots and potatoes.

When Jackpile opened up
on Laguna land, some Laguna men got on alright,
at the bottom.
You have to start at the bottom, personnel said,
for a training period and work your way up.
The Acoma men went to the Ambrosia Lake mines
and always got stuck by the space
on the application forms
for previous mining experience,
but the mine steward explained,
You have to start at the bottom
and work your way up.

So, it's almost thirty years later,
and the Acoma men
are at the bottom
of the underground mines at Ambrosia Lake,
and the Laguna men
are at the bottom of the open pit at Jackpile,
and they're still training, gaining experience,
and working their way up.

And weekends, that city jail
is still full.[1]

—Simon Ortiz, "Starting at the Bottom"

Remember the Past, Dream the Future: A Theology of Liberation and Healing

The particular bondage of American Indian peoples presents peculiar difficulties for identifying an appropriate starting point for writing an American Indian theology. We are faced, on the one hand, with a broad spectrum of the rich diversity of Indian mythological expressions and other traditional narratives, forms of Indian spirituality, ceremonies, and structures of Indian societies. Each of the hundreds of indigenous nations of North America has its own discrete cultural and social structures that would provide for a very interesting theological reflection and would capture the imagination of many a reader, perhaps especially readers external to the American Indian community.[2]

On the other hand, the contemporary Native American experience of disintegration and alienation derives from the ongoing history of conquest, oppression, and poverty, with all of their ongoing consequences. Thus, two different expectations of an Indian theology function—one characterized by euro-american desires for the exotic other of Indianness as a New Age spiritual delectable, the other characterized by Indian poverty and need. If a theology is to be a part of a people's life-giving, life-sustaining social structure, it dare not just be interesting, especially just interesting to an external audience. Rather, a Native American theology must not only speak out of Native American experience and culture, but also speak to the contemporary reality of Native American existence. Yet to begin with our traditional spiritual base, it could be argued, would do more than interest external readers. After more than five hundred years of colonialism and conquest, so much of those old native traditions has been lost or sublimated in Indian communities that to rehearse them in a Native American theology could serve some legitimately useful purpose for Indian people.

As acute as is the dissolution of Indian culture and spirituality, the recovery of religious traditions is not our first need today. Indeed, a question that precedes reclaiming our rightful cultural and spiritual heritage has to do with why the particulars of that heritage have been suppressed, repressed, and even lost in so many cases across the continent. More to the point, any attempt to write a Native American theology must speak to Indian peoples about the present context of the peoples' oppression and alienation. Thus, an Indian theology must begin with the present-day social disintegration experienced by every Indian community, and begin to name the causes for the disintegration.

It is not even enough to recognize the loss of ancestral spiritual traditions, because we have lost much more than stories and ceremonies. The very social fabric that once held our communities together has been shredded by the continuing events of the european conquest. Whether they are in traditional reservation-based communities or new urban communities, American Indian people today exhibit dramatic levels of dysfunction in all aspects of personal and community existence. Poverty and oppression, caused by the conquest and the continuing need for an immigrant population to repress any expression of Indian self-determination or autonomy, have resulted in American Indian people suffering disproportionately as the most distressed ethnic community in North America, as measured by an array of social well-being statistics.[3] Compared with the total U.S. population, American Indians endure rates of unemployment, alcoholism, suicides, and homicide that are from 40 percent to 600 percent higher, and rates of longevity, levels of education attained, proportions of school dropouts, and levels of income that are significantly (10 percent to 50 percent) less than the general population.[4]

This situation reasonably requires that a Native American theology begin with this context as political reality and move quickly to press for a new vision of health and well-being (what some might call salvation) for the people. Thus, an American Indian theology must be a theology of liberation. It must be overtly political. This American Indian theology will begin with a clear memory of how we got where we are today in order that we might begin to create a future that is healthier than our present. Traditional Indian ways of thinking become important in the process as well. Hence, the title of this section has a traditional meaning: We remember the past in order to dream the future, in order to dream or imagine the future into existence, just as Spider Woman thought the world into existence in the act of creation.[5]

One key starting point in this process of remembering and dreaming is that it must be clearly identified as an Indian process. Our liberation, our healing, depends on our not allowing someone else to remember or dream on our behalf. To the extent that our remembered past is filled with five hundred years of memories of genocide and oppression that have left Indian peoples with emotional, spiritual, and social wounds that continue to fester, we must also remember that our past and our future have been consistently signified for us— by missionaries, by anthropologists and other university academics, by government bureaucrats, etc.[6] In the interests of liberation and self-determination, Indian people must now take the healing of Indian communities into their own hands. After all this time, it should be abundantly clear, to Indian and non-Indian, that Indian people can count on neither the U.S. government, nor the churches of the United States, nor the private-sector institutions of free enterprise to solve any of the problems that these institutions have invested so much time in creating.[7] As Indian people begin to identify the social dysfunction of Indian communities, it is becoming clearer to us that the healing of Indian communities is Indian business, to be conducted by Indian people and Indian community organizations in a way that is consistent with Indian cultures and values.

White American Healing:
Remember the Past and Dream the Future

The creation of this Native American theology cannot stop at this point, however. While I have written as an American Indian theologian primarily for American Indian communities, I must also keep in mind non-Indian readers, especially White, euro-american, and other euro-western readers, who will look to this book for some clue to the healing of their own community. Moreover, it is increasingly clear that the social and, for instance, the ecological dysfunction of the White world and the "world system" it has generated is fully "codependent" with Indian dysfunction, and that our healing must be somehow linked with the healing of the european and euro-american community. In other words, while the internal healing of American Indian communities may be Indian business at one level, any real healing or liberation in the world of American Indians must be paralleled by healing in the world of euro-americans in order for the healing of Indian peoples to be sustained. Hence, at some point, this Indian theology of liberation must speak to the possibility of the liberation of euro-americans from their past and toward a future of hope.

The liberation of euro-american peoples must be rooted in some sort of *systemic* confession and repentance with respect to their relationship with the native peoples of this continent. To call this confession systemic suggests clearly that, for once, euro-american social structures must rise above the radical individualism of the western intellectual tradition. This is to say that feelings of individual guilt in this process will generally not help generate substantive change. To the contrary, both individual and corporate feelings of guilt can even generate defensiveness and denial, to use a term common in therapeutic addictions recovery.[8] Rather, a more helpful, proactive response is necessary for owning the corporate past and imagining a new future.

For instance, one often hears descendants of euro-american immigrants insist, "I did not do anything to American Indian peoples. All that history of atrocities happened long ago—long before I was born. Can we not let bygones be bygones and go on from here?" There are two immediate problems with this sort of denial. First, it conveniently ignores the fact that the immigrant descendants have consistently benefited from the atrocities committed by their ancestors while native descendants continue to experience the resulting deprivation. Rather than ask whether immigrant descendants should have to pay the price for their ancestors' atrocities, a more constructive question might ask why American Indian heirs must pay the price for the oppression earlier euro-americans inflicted on our Indian ancestors. The second point is correlative to the first: Contemporary euro-american occupation of Indian land is an important continuing benefit of the conquest that must be accounted for in the euro-american moral and spiritual inventory. In euro-american legal discourse, a recipient of stolen property is just as liable as the actual thief. To say that it happened so long ago that it should no longer matter is a wholly inadequate conception of justice. Moreover, because of the consistent development of "White privilege," even those euro-western immigrants who came to the United States after the conquest of Indian lands and resources was completed continue to benefit from the conquest itself in countless ways, including a higher socioeconomic status.[9]

Another aspect of this problem that deserves attention is that the "history of atrocities" did not just happen long ago in the past. The history of oppression of American Indian peoples is a continuing saga in America that will probably not end anytime soon. At a gross, surface structure level, the continuing oppression can be tracked in the news media in terms of the Dann sisters and the Western Shoshone struggle to reclaim legitimate title to their land from the U.S. government in Nevada; the role of the U.S. government in creating the struggle of Navajo and Hopi peoples over Big Mountain in Arizona; the catholic church's role in the construction of an observatory on the top of Mount Graham, an Apache sacred site, also in Arizona; the Sioux nation's continuing struggle to reclaim the Black Hills; and countless other aboriginal land claim cases.[10] The mining of radioactive minerals on Indian land provides another insight into the ongoing oppression, as does the attempt to locate radioactive and other toxic wastes on Indian lands under the guise of economic development. It should not go unnoticed that some 70 percent of uranium resources in North America are on Indian land and that access to these resources is considered a national security issue. This means that Indian self-determination on reservations where these deposits are located is effectively nullified in relation to Indian decision making with regard to these mineral resources.[11]

Sovereignty and Sustainable Development: The Indian Future

Essentially, then, a Native American theology must be a liberation theology and a theology of resistance, and as such, it must speak out of its uniquely indigenous context. Thus, it must begin and end its spiritual journey with political analysis. The remainder of this chapter points to two correlative political issues that affect the well-being of Indian peoples and Indian cultures. The first issue is American Indian national sovereignty;[12] the second is the modern debate on sustainable development, initiated by the UN's Brundtland Report[13] and the United Nations Conference on Environment and Development held in Rio de Janeiro in 1992.[14] Ultimately, sustainable development is merely a liberal argument for development and reaffirms the persistence of the temporal notion of progress. I would prefer to argue for sustainable stasis as an option for indigenous national communities and, at the least, argue for assured sustainability—quite separate from the added hook of "development"—for all small, culturally integrous communities.

Sovereignty as Liberation

The question of sovereignty has to do not just with issues of the autonomy of a people or with some vague or indeterminate notion of self-determination. Sovereignty must include the international recognition of a people qua people. Autonomy and self-determination are critical parameters of international recognition and are essential to the international validating process.[15] There is, however, an impediment to this process. Namely, the political and economic bias in the international discourse is to recognize only *states* as the fundamental actors in international political discourse. As such, the natural national entities that make up indigenous peoples' communities are seen today as merely ethnic minorities within state structures, who may have individual rights but who do not have any distinct set of community or cultural rights as an independent people.[16] Hence, the sovereignty or autonomy of indigenous *nations* is a priori bracketed from consideration in any state discourse.[17]

The recent history of Yanomami peoples in the rain forest of Venezuela and Brazil serves as an example. Following their first encounter with euroamericans in the 1960s, the Yanomami have been decimated by subjugation, dislocation, and violent death, including several massacres at the hands of the invaders of their homelands.[18] The situation of indigenous peoples in the rain forest is comparable in much of equatorial South America, including Peru, Paraguay, Ecuador, and Colombia. It is a rather complex causal nexus. First of all, the West has a world environmental concern for, not to say a self-interest in, the rain forest—these ecosystems are the lungs of the world. Replenishing the world oxygen supply depends on jungle photosynthesis. However, Brazil, Peru, and other South American states perceive a pressing economic need to develop—that is, cut down—the rain forest. The need is intensified and exacerbated by the debt these countries owe to financial institutions in the United States, Europe, and Japan.

There is yet another significant step, a part of the post-1492 systemic whole. Around 1492, the divine right of kings began to give way to the divine right of the nation-state.[19] Since then, the sovereignty of states has been assumed a priori as sovereignty over both peoples and territories. Hence, Brazil and Peru assume state sovereignty over their rain forest territories. However, the rain forest is and has been inhabited by peoples who have lived there for thousands of years, have been largely unaffected by the existence of Brazil or Peru until very recently, have known nothing of those states' claims to territorial sovereignty over the lands they have inhabited uninterrupted and undisturbed until now, and certainly have not ceded their own sovereignty to one or the other of these states.

Yet the international prioritization of the sovereignty of states and the world system economic structures apply constant pressure on these "developing" countries to conform to other state partners in the international arena. Brazil, Peru, and others have had to systemically assume the territorial prerogatives of state sovereignty that dare not acknowledge any hint of indigenous sovereignty or even any extensive acknowledgment that these communities have rights to their own lands.[20]

The liberation of American Indian and other indigenous peoples requires both an external (international) and self-acknowledgment of our peopleness. Sustainability must begin with affirmation of existing ancient nations and continue with the struggle to establish those nations as sustainable communities. The questions for political theory as a discipline are these: At what point and by what process did a people who never ceded their sovereignty to an immigrant colonial state lose their sovereign status to these modern state entities? And what is the moral reasoning that sustains such exercises of state sovereignty?[21] If political theory is so severely limited by economic expediency and cannot address the moral issue involved here, then our theologies must. At some point we must draw a line in the sand and acknowledge that these people are people, that their aboriginal and ancient rights to the land are indeed legitimate rights that precede any notion of state sovereignty.

Commencing with the Universal Declaration of Human Rights adopted by the United Nations in 1948, several developments in the arena of international law have effectively marginalized and eroded the capabilities of minority groups to achieve status as self-determined nations or peoples and thereby to enjoy political currency among existing states. The central theme in these developments is the increased privileging of the *individual's* human rights as there has been an increase in the number of immigrant and refugee claimants seeking mediation through international human rights codes and covenants. These efforts are consistent with the liberal projects imposed on American Indians for the last 150 years. The individual has become "an object of law and a site for rights,"[22] at the apparent cost of the sovereign rights of indigenous nations. Pressed by the delegates representing states, the June 1993 human rights gathering in Vienna chose to deal with indigenous rights in a fashion that finally denies group rights in favor of affirming (euro-western) individual rights to all people. Thus, in these cases, they finally distinguished between human rights and right to sovereignty. The major international human rights discussion of our time chose to continue to impose unjust theories of sovereignty on peoples who never did cede their own rights to anyone else.[23]

"Sustainable Development": An Oxymoron?

This chapter addresses the issue of autonomy within the question of sustainable development. The ensuing discussion will highlight the cultural inappropriateness of the whole sustainable development discourse to Indian and other indigenous peoples and will begin to address the cultural/spiritual traditions of Indian peoples that might speak to the question in a persuasive way. In the latter, we begin to get at explicitly theological concerns.

Since the UN's Brundtland Report and the 1992 Rio Earth Summit, any number of institutions from the World Bank[24] to the World Council of Churches[25] and many national denominations have rushed to create units addressing the question of sustainable development. By and large, sustainable development has been seen as a two-part strategy: First, it is a development strategy intended to take the threat of environmental degradation seriously. Second, it is interpreted by many as a strategy for mitigating the negative effects of the more usual sorts of development that have been generated by the economic power centers of the West and imposed on the poorer, developing states of the South.[26] The history of the imposition of western, developmental economics on Indian peoples and other indigenous nations and the prospects for something called sustainable development raise essential theological and socioeconomic questions. While the development paradigm designed and implemented over the past forty years has resulted in mal-development for Third and Fourth World peoples, the introduction of the language of "sustainable development" continues some of the same problems.[27]

Sustainable Development or Mal-Development?

Ideologies of "civilization" and "development" have been the consistent liberal euro-american and european remedies to the genocide, chaos, and dysfunction wrought by the european invasions of indigenous societies ongoing for more than 500 years.[28] A critical aspect of the development strategy, as implicated in Simon Ortiz's poem at the beginning of this chapter, has been primarily economic, bestowing on our nations gifts of mining operations (from coal and oil to the uranium he mentions at Acoma and Laguna); land-leasing procedures imposed on people by the Bureau of Indian Affairs; a variety of penny-ante tribal enterprises like tobacco shops, fish farming, and small resorts; and toxic waste storage on Indian reservation lands.[29] Needless to say, this sort of development has not usually worked to the benefit of Indian communities, although it has empowered and enriched a few quislings among every nation who have sold out their communities in order to work the system for personal

gain, financially and politically. Some estimates of American Indian unemployment suggest that nationally Indian people suffer unemployment at a real
rate of 50 or 60 percent—this in spite of attempts of development in every
Indian community.[30]

Indian communities have also experienced something that smacks of "sustainable development," but the track record has been less than salutary. From
nearly the beginning, from Bartolomé de Las Casas in the south to John Eliot
in the north, seemingly well-intentioned missionaries and government officials have engaged in activities that might be classified under sustainable
development's notions of "human development." For instance, education,
especially reading and writing, has been consistently at the top of the list.
Indeed, european and euro-american liberals, explicitly or implicitly touched
by some religious motivation, took seriously the "civilization" of Indian people,
whether said people wanted to be civilized or not.[31] The result was the consistent imposition of european cultural values, norms, societal structures, and
technologies on peoples who had lived remarkably well with their own values,
norms, structures, and technologies for some thousands of years.

The disruption caused by such "sustainable development" or "human
development" has nearly destroyed Indian communities across what is now
the continental United States. It has left us with intense societal and individual functional disabilities. Moreover, liberality and good intentions to the contrary, this sort of "sustainable development" turned out to be merely a part of
the conquest, even if, like Las Casas, it searched for a more gentle way to con-
quer.[32] Our experience with development is that it changes who we are by
changing our culture, social structures, even the structures of our families.
Most notably, this ongoing "development" project, which has been and is still
being imposed on Indian people, destroys the communitarian values and
structures of Indian nations and replaces them with individualistic values and
social structures that conform to the cultural norms of dominant power structures. Invariably, development, even so-called human development, has left
devastation and confusion in its wake.

While this mal-development process of civilizing continues to this day, it is
more common that American Indian and other indigenous peoples experience
an exclusion from the decision-making process in the political arena of development negotiations. While churches may occasionally pay attention, states
are far more likely to ignore indigenous peoples in planning development
strategies, except perhaps as potential pools of cheap labor. Thus, in the ten-
sion between the North and South, between the rich and powerful states and
the poor, so-called developing countries, an important segment of the world's
population is lost. It does not seem to matter whether indigenous populations

live in the North or South, one of the keys to state development in either context is exploitation and oppression of indigenous peoples, first of all with regard to access to indigenous land and natural resources. The poverty of southern, developing states, for example, exacerbates the crisis of indigenous nations, since the state claims de jure a sovereignty that supersedes the natural and agelong sovereignty of all indigenous nations, including national territories, within the existing state borders. Moreover, any genuine acknowledgment of the claims of indigenous communities within its borders would potentially impede the state's freedom to develop land and resources over which it claims sovereignty. While this represents something of a catch-22 for indigenous nations and southern states of poor people, development strategies always have more negative and destructive effects on native peoples and their communities. Additionally, development strategies always represent a continued pressure on indigenous nations—pressure to compromise further national sovereignty.[33]

The results of development policies and programs in the international arena have to this point been painfully dismal. The planners of these programs have, at best, only a hint of the suffering their remedies have caused. For the moment, I think we need to bypass the "how" of sustainable development and instead focus on the "why." To analyze the validity of the entire concept of sustainable development, we must first ask probing questions about world history post-1492 to better understand how we arrived at this dilemma in the first place. We must ask who really benefits and who in fact gets hurt in development projects, whether they are launched with dishonest intentions, as described in Ortiz's poem, or pursued with genuine concern and integrity. We must also, in this analysis, ask probing questions about the worldview of euroamericans, which is inherently the driving force of the entire notion of development. Vandana Shiva observes that the scientific and industrial revolutions abetted the europeans' project to colonize nature just as they colonized the many lands and cultures of the world: "'Nature' was transformed in the european mind from a self-organizing, living system to a mere raw material for human exploitation, needing management and control."[34] Integral to the colonizer's plan to claim *all* the resources with the least amount of trouble was/is the determination that the indigenous peoples of the area were/are in fact *a part of the natural landscape,* a "part of the fauna."[35] Development projects become the vehicles to impose these worldviews on other cultures, despite earnest protests from participants that this is not the case.

I am not an economist nor a political theorist, but rather a theologian who is unequivocally committed to the well-being and liberation of my own (American Indian) community. As a result, I necessarily pay attention to issues of

economics, law, political theory, and international relations as they affect the
community for whom I reflect theologically. I will venture one other predispo-
sition: A people's mythology and their theological reflection on it precedes and
helps determine much of the particularity of their social, economic, and political structure, whether their foundational mythology is American Indian,
judeo-christian, or humanist/scientific method.

The whole notion of "development" is an idea that people in Third and
Fourth World contexts, including those contexts within the borders of the
United States, regularly experience as the reality of mal-development.[36] I do
intend the oxymoronic self-contradiction implied in the term *mal-development*.
I must necessarily applaud any attempt to reconceive development in terms
that put the well-being of human beings before the oversimplified insistence
that the well-being of the economic engine translates at some point into well-
being for people. At the same time, it is necessary to critique the notion of "sustainable development" as still perpetuating the imposition of a euro-american
cultural frame of reference on the rest of the world.

Much of what is being written about sustainable development, especially
by various church units, repeatedly treats the present as a time of crisis and
presses the question "How far-reaching are the necessary changes?"[37] I want
to press for a vision that sees the need for deep and fundamental social and
structural change. I want to argue for radical and creative vision that will ultimately change the way we live together on this planet. I will not settle for a
vision that merely intends to "fix" the system that now dominates the globe. It
is not fixable and must give way to a new and fresh vision. I want to take seriously the pronouncement by the Presbyterian Church's Task Force on Sustainable Development in *The Sustainability-Development Debate* that "It may
be that God is leading the church and the world to something quite new—to
changes in policy and practice, system and lifestyle, that will be difficult and
costly but finally fulfilling, for earth and people in renewed community."[38]
Indeed, rationality itself should be leading us to something new. My argument
builds around the following ten points:

1. Western, european, and euro-american cultures—in spite of demonstra-
ble strengths—have a nearly fatal flaw (Forbes: *wetiko*),[39] which has generated
the present crisis.[40] While this flaw is most apparent today in political and economic relationships in the world, its underlying sources are the spiritual, theological, mythological, and philosophical imaginations of the West. In other
places I have described these in terms of the overwhelming mythological commitment of the West to individualism and temporality.[41]

2. A growth analysis (development or sustainable development, human
expenditure ratios, basic human needs, etc.) may not be the most effective way

to understand and resolve the current (economic, environmental, developmental) crisis. A growth analysis, first of all, is quintessentially western in its cognitive structure, wholly given over to temporality and progress in its discourse. Moreover, since in every case the developmental problem that is identified is essentially rooted in a political context that has generated the problem, it would make more sense to engage first of all in a *political power analysis*. Who has the power? Where does it come from? How is that power used to further disempower those with less advantage? How can communities be empowered once again to take care of themselves? Rather than reduce these questions to questions of economics first of all, a power analysis will allow economics to fall into place as one aspect of the discussion. We must start with an analysis of the political power and authority a small, local community has or does not have to make its own decisions with regard to how it will live its communal life.

3. The use of the word *development* in the construct *sustainable development* already represents a cultural imposition on American Indian and other indigenous peoples. The word is charged from the beginning of the discussion with the imposed bias that the critical category of cognition is temporal and presumes that all peoples have a self-perceived need and desire to develop something. For peoples whose cultural integrity, worldview, and mythology are oriented spatially and whose societal ideal is a stasis of balance and harmony, a genocidal compromise in their cultural integrity is immediately indicated. Yet the vision of both the experts from western cultural contexts and statist-oriented Third World actors in the international arena is limited by their cultural commitment to temporality and the dictates of perceived economic forces that always function temporally in the modern world system.[42] For the rest of us, sustainable development is an oxymoron, one that will finally function to destroy indigenous cultures and is probably doomed to global failure.

4. The heart of the current crisis is rooted in the five-hundred-year emergence of the modern state, coinciding with Europe's conquest of the Americas. The state is a modern and artificial political entity marked by the acute centralization of authority over arbitrarily determined larger territories and populations in large bureaucratic organisms whose primary objective invariably seems to be the sustainable development of itself.[43] In political science, the assumption has always been that the state represents the nation and vice versa. Yet the move toward larger, centralized states means implicitly that the growth of the state hinges on the usurping of nations whose existence had been originally independent of any state. Thus, states are rarely homogeneous.

5. Modern state borders are also artificial and unnatural. This is most pronounced in post- (neo-) colonial contexts such as in Africa, where modern

state boundaries conform to former european colonial holdings and totally disregard ancient national realities, and India, which claims sovereignty over one half of the Naga Nation (Nagalim) in extreme northeast India, while the other half is claimed as a part of the state of Myanmar.[44] On the one hand, natural national entities are typically divided by modern borders. On the other, nations are thrown together in these modern states in ways that create political and economic imbalance as one national group tries to or succeeds in dominating the others. We need to move toward recognizing natural boundaries and natural national entities.

6. Rather than engaging in and assisting outside "experts" in development projects, the real task for the world's marginalized indigenous peoples is to reclaim natural boundaries and national entities, which would begin to meet a fundamental need of American Indian and other indigenous peoples for what is variously described as sovereignty, autonomy, or self-determination. No Indian nation, my own included, ever technically ceded its sovereignty to a government of the United States or agreed to its sovereignty being superseded by that of this artificial political entity called the United States. Rather, the United States, under the leadership of the liberal Republican Indian affairs reform movement of the 1860s and 1870s, acted unilaterally to accomplish this act.[45]

7. Ultimately, I would like to see a vision emerge in the world of small, local, autonomous communities as the basic political unit recognized and respected by everyone, with tolerance for a wide variety of politically organized configurations.

8. Cultural integrity, community worldview, and communal sets of values cannot allow for simply replacing one dominating world system with another equally imposed on all people. Thus, American Indians and other indigenous peoples have rarely had any lasting interest in marxism or any other euro-western forms of sociopolitical universalism.[46]

9. There is something fundamental to a culture and its community (a variable from culture to culture) that generates different attitudes toward nature, including toward other peoples. One culture ought not dominate or impose values on others. Indeed, the economically more powerful culture may not be the more powerful culture spiritually and morally.

10. Native American cultures, functioning out of a communitarian base and oriented fundamentally toward spatiality rather than temporality, may have something radically creative and salvific to say to all of us in this crisis. While autonomy is really the beginning point both for an American Indian theology and for the health and well-being (salvation) of the Indian commu-

nity, I would argue that there is benefit to all in the world, developed states included, in recognizing the inherent sovereignty of American Indian and other indigenous peoples.

Greed and Euro-American Economics

About twenty years ago, I read a letter sent by General William T. Sherman, commander of the U.S. Army Division of the West, to the U.S. War Department. The Civil War was over, and the United States was then being badly beaten by Red Cloud and the Lakotas in the Powder River War.[47] With a note of resignation, Sherman conceded that it would take much longer than anticipated to achieve the liberal Republican goal of civilizing these Indians. His analysis concluded that the Indians "know no greed, and, until they understand greed, they will never understand the private ownership of property."[48] As is usually the case with White interpreters of Indian culture and values, Sherman had only a superficial understanding of Indian people. As a result, his quote is more revealing with respect to White, euro-american culture than it is about Indian people. Indeed, that world system, which evolved out of Europe's conquest of the Americas and was already firmly established by Sherman's day, was predicated precisely on the institutionalization of individualized greed as a motivating force.

Where Sherman's analysis falls short is in his characterization of Indian peoples as knowing no greed. I would argue to the contrary that Indian people certainly did understand the human emotions and motivations of greed, but had powerful and complex social mechanisms for systemically suppressing them in the interest of a communal sense of wholeness and well-being. It is not, then, that American Indian peoples have been unable to understand the basics of the capitalist, developmentalist system that has dominated the world since 1492; rather, American Indian societies have had no cultural room for that fundamental ingredient, greed, which fires up the whole capitalist system. Where Sherman's analysis is useful is in highlighting how antithetical Indian cultural values are to the values inculcated in euro-american culture by the post-1492 world system. Temporality and individualism are laced throughout the history of the western tradition in its theology, philosophy, and finally economic theory. Economics assumes that people universally aspire to individualistic self-maximizing acquisition, so this discipline has functioned to institutionalize human greed as fundamental to the economic engine of the world system.[49]

Foundations of an Alternative Vision

Native American societies universally use stories and ceremonial acts to undergird a worldview that is fundamentally different from all cultural worldviews that have been able to function "successfully" in the modern world system's economy. For instance, many of the Coyote/Culture Hero stories identify the motivating force of greed, but do so in ways that clearly identify it as a source of evil and destruction within the community. Story after story teaches Indian young to eschew personal gratification and to strive for the good of the whole community instead. At times Coyote is the negative, paradigmatic model of that base human nature we expect our children to strive to avoid. Then in other stories even Coyote is able to overcome his base selfish nature to work for the good of the whole (community, nation, and world).[50]

Like the Culture Hero stories, the mythologies of Indian peoples also teach the foundational importance of communitarian values and the destructiveness of greed and self-aggrandizement. These mythologies form the foundation of all American Indian theological reflection and the social structures and communal patterns of behavior that follow.

Nationally specific examples would include the Blackfoot story of the origin of tobacco and the Lakota story of the brothers who heroically killed Uncegila, the river monster:

> In the Blackfoot story, it is said that Creator gave this sacred tobacco plant to four brothers for them to share with the people, in order to empower their prayers and help give them greater clarity of vision. The four, however, choose to keep the plant to themselves, thus empowering only themselves and elevating themselves among the people. Any spiritual (medical, social, economic, emotional, etc.) help needed by anyone in the community can be provided only by these four brothers. Only they know the ceremonies, stories, and songs to make the medicine strong. Moreover, they conceal the field where they planted the tobacco, keeping the whole process a secret.
>
> One couple know this to be a perversion, know that the weed is to be shared by all and is a gift intended to empower the whole community. Committed to the discovery of tobacco and all its attendant ceremonies, this husband and wife go out together on a spiritual journey to bring tobacco back to all the people. In a lengthy story involving several days of valiant but unsuccessful attempts on the part of the man, the narrative finally revolves

around the woman and her discovery of a beaver lodge. As the two of them make an opening in the lodge, they make contact with the beavers who live there and explain their quest to these relatives. Since tobacco is a "water" medicine, the beavers are indeed able to help. Turning themselves into human forms, they come to the lodge of the couple and begin to teach them everything about tobacco—the planting, the ceremony, the songs, etc., all retold in the story in great detail. At this point, even the telling of the story becomes a teaching device to younger members of the community, teaching them both the agronomy involved and the ceremony.

Finally, with seeds in hand, the couple set out to plant tobacco. In this first planting, things progress very quickly, so that in a matter of some four days, the tobacco has reached maturity. Then the story takes an ironically punitive twist. Just as they are ready to harvest their first batch of tobacco, a huge hailstorm devastates the countryside, destroying the four brothers' tobacco field but leaving the couple's field unscathed. The brothers, who failed to retain seed for future plantings, are wiped out. Hearing rumors to the effect that the couple have successfully found and cultivated tobacco, the brothers rush to intercede, promising to take the couple in, as it were, as partners, thereby maintaining their monopoly on power in the community. It is, however, too late. With the harvest in, the couple have already distributed both tobacco and seed to all in the community.

Suddenly, the community is restored to some sense of parity. Balance and harmony are restored for the moment. Individual greed and acquisition of power and goods have been thwarted. And every hearer of the story learns anew the importance of community-based living and acting. All are taught to resist the temptations of personal greed.[51]

The Lakota story of the two brothers who slay *uncegila*, the water monster, takes a different tack. In this story, the monster is an external hindrance to the well-being of the community. It is the presence of capricious evil in the people's world. The story includes a glorification of the warrior ideal, with the promise of untold power to anyone who rids the people of this pestilence. The activity of the warrior at the time of combat, like the hunt, is one of the necessary breaks from the ideal of a community in the stasis of balance and harmony. While many tried to defeat *uncegila*, none succeeded, but rather paid

the price for their bravery with their lives. Even looking at and seeing the monster, it is reported, means immediate and painful death to any human being.
This fact alone accounts for all previous failures.

> Two brothers, one of them blind, set out on this adventure. They
> assume that between them, with sacred arrows provided by an
> old woman who lives alone in the woods, they can succeed. The
> story develops at some length the relationship between the blind
> brother and the old woman, who becomes transformed into a
> young beauty as he makes love to her. She, in turn, gives the
> brothers some instruction on how to take care of the beast when
> they have killed it. When the journey continues, the brothers
> plan a strategy for their hunt. While the seeing brother functions
> as the eyes for the other, they decide, the blind one will do the
> shooting, since the arrows are sacred and will not miss their
> mark. Just as the monster is to make its appearance from the
> water, the seeing brother averts his eyes, and they both count to
> seven, giving the monster time to rise up fully out of the water.
> Then the blind brother shoots his arrows, each one hitting the
> seventh spot at the base of the monster's neck, successfully
> killing the monster.
>
> The brothers continue to complete all the instructions given
> to them by the beautiful young woman, avoiding each of the pre-
> dicted pitfalls that would bring the monster back to life again.
> Finally, according to instructions, they build a lodge over a deep
> pit that will contain the heart of the beast. From that time on,
> their task is to take care of the day-to-day needs of the heart,
> feeding it and completing daily ceremonies. In return, they
> become immensely powerful—as hunters, warriors, lovers, in all
> things. All they do is successful; they are revered by all in the
> community for their heroism and success. All the women, even
> the married women, work to seduce the two of them so that they
> are never in want for the pleasures of a companion. Even the one
> brother's blindness was healed by the heart.
>
> The two brothers become bored with success. They finally
> agree that they crave being like other people in the community
> and that they have come to dislike their special powers. Even the
> variety of sexual companions, they decide, is boring. So they
> decide to do the one thing the beautiful woman told them not to
> do. This act will destroy the power of the heart that was given to

them. To destroy the heart, they invite the rest of the community into the secret lodge that contains the heart in the pit, and they allow everyone to look at the heart. As predicted, the onlookers' gaze destroys the heart, and the brothers are reduced once again to common people.[52]

The point of the story, similar to that of the tobacco story, is to warn hearers, especially young hearers, away from selfish acts of greed-induced desire. Be careful, is the message, what you desire may not be what you expect it to be. It is better to be one with the people. Here is a story of two men who were more gifted and capable than anyone alive today. Yet even they found that the special individual powers given to them for their successes were too much for them to enjoy. Work instead for the good of the people, and be happy to be a common person (*ikce wicsa, ikce winyan*).

Both stories function to limit the effects of human individual desire and greed, in order to build the good of the whole. The community comes always before the individual. While stature and importance are typically measured in the West by the individual accumulation of wealth (along with its corollary, power), stature in the Indian world is more readily measured by how much one has "given away." Indeed, more than one missionary chastised the ritual giveaway of Indian societies as diabolical and anti-christian. Today development proponents would see the tradition of giveaway as a quaint anachronism diametrically opposed to their perceived virtues of development.[53] Yet in my own tribe, election to the Council of Little Old Ones, the ruling elders of the community, depended in part on such a track record of generosity. One could not be considered for such an office unless one had literally given away all that one had at least four times during one's life. In such a context, capitalism not only becomes difficult to conceive or understand, but flies directly in the face of the structure of values that the society holds to and which bring life to the society.

Indigenous values go beyond generosity. Violence cannot be perpetrated, a life taken, in a Native American society, without some spiritual act of reciprocation. I am so much a part of the whole of creation and its balance, anything I do to perpetrate an act of violence, even a necessary act of violence like hunting or harvesting, must be accompanied by an act of spiritual reciprocation intended to restore the balance of existence. Hence hunting and war typically involved a ceremonial preparation before a contingent of warriors left their home. The Osage war ceremony, for instance, involved an twelve-day ritual—time to affirm the sacredness of life, to consecrate the lives that would be lost in war, and to offer prayers in reciprocation for those potentially lost lives.[54] In the hunt, most Indian nations report specified prayers of reciprocation, involving apologies and words of thanksgiving to the animal itself and the animal's spirit nation. Usually, this ceremonial act complies with the request of the animals themselves as the people remember their primordial negotiations in mythological stories.[55] Even after the hunt or battle, those who participated must invariably go through a ceremonial cleansing before reentering their own village. To overlook this would bring the disruption of the sacred caused by the perpetration of violence right into the middle of national life and put all people at risk.[56] The ideal of harmony and balance requires that all share a respect for all other existent things, a respect for life and avoiding gratuitous or unthinking acts of violence. Maintaining harmony and balance requires that even necessary acts of violence be done, as traditional Indians would say, "in a sacred way."

No model of development, as far as I know, embodies or incorporates indigenous ethics of generosity or reciprocity as they are found in Indian communities. It is not enough to replant a few trees or add nutrients to the soil. These are superficial acts to treat the negative symptoms of development. The value of reciprocity, which is a hallmark of Indian ceremonies, goes to the heart of issues of sustainability—that is, maintaining a balance and tempering the negative effects of basic human survival techniques.

The sustainable development documents speak of limits; Indian ceremonies are an eloquent expression of the wisdom of living within limits. Although the sustainable development documents address the issue of limits, they revolve around some basic assumptions and worldviews that are diametrically opposed to those of indigenous communities.[57] Inherent in the Indian worldview of harmony and balance is a deep understanding of the need for human limits in order to maintain the harmony and balance of all creation. For indigenous peoples, *not* all things are possible for humans, because some human actions (for example, mining uranium or cutting down rain forests) would destroy the balance of the world.

Contrary to the indigenous view, the ethos of development strategies, including sustainable development, is that human beings have unlimited potential, which it is somehow *un*ethical *not* to utilize and/or exploit. In other words, development proponents would say that if it can be done, it should be done so that *human beings* will benefit. There is an emphasis on fulfillment of human potential,[58] but the goal is to enable individuals to fit into an anthropocentric world system rather than a creation-centered world system. There is not a core value of balance with other created beings, which would set limits on otherwise unlimited human potential. Sustainable development proponents add some superficial language about limits without abandoning the core value of augmenting or exploiting human potential, regardless of the cost to the health and balance of creation.

More than merely demonstrating a difference of opinion about how the world functions, the disparity between western development/modernization views and indigenous views results in serious and often deadly consequences for the marginalized and powerless indigenous communities. Any notion of development predicates a shift in worldview away from traditional indigenous notions of the common good and harmony and balance of the universe, toward a temporal, linear, progress-oriented worldview in some way modeled by the european and american West. Hence, it would seem that development, perhaps even "sustainable development," requires a capitulation to genocide on the part of indigenous peoples. More to the point, the compromise stands to cost the world community a set of lived cultural values that may be the key to world survival.[59]

Empowering Real National Communities

To explain the objection to development strategies, it is necessary to outline some issues of social organization. In introducing the concept of small, local, autonomous communities, I am both building on and arguing against the notions Benedict Anderson introduces in his book *Imagined Communities*.[60] I am offering an opposite configuration to his thesis, preferring to recapture something of the premodern, pre-1492 world as a vision of a postpostmodern existence. I want to argue for a breaking down of the old borders, more or less artificially established after 1492. The small, locally autonomous communities I envision would constitute something of a reemergence of a smaller-scale, local autonomy similar to those that were more common in the world before the emergence of large, centralized, authoritarian state structures, perhaps beginning with the rule of Henry VII in England[61] or, more symbolically, with the marriage of Ferdinand and Isabella and the uniting of the feudal fiefdoms of Castile and Aragon in what then became Spain.[62]

I fully understand that my vision introduces significant modern problems with respect to how the world might work with the existence of so many smaller economies, currencies, markets, all resulting from multitudes of communities claiming autonomy. Yet it is critical that we envision other possibilities for social/political configurations. To plan elaborate development strategies before considering other possible forms of social organization (which have in the past proved quite successful) is to confine our range of solutions within boundaries that have already proven their flaws. Attendant to the recovery and implementation of a pre-columbian community model would be the actualization of socioeconomic structures and relationships that require relatively few of the adjudicatory or policing mechanisms—which are both requisite and numerous in western societies—owing to a cosmology centered on harmony and balance.

While the problems are imposing, small indigenous communities did indeed have shared markets and shared technologies, which were at least pancontinental. Small, locally autonomous communities were able to retain their autonomy and self-determination while at the same time having far-reaching trade and contact with other indigenous cultures. These communities existed within geographical regions and retained their autonomy within these regions; the regions were not in themselves autonomous. Rather, autonomy existed at a more intimate, more local level. Goods from Costa Rica were most likely not traded as far north as Minnesota. It is important to ask at what point that link was lost and why competition did not enter the dynamic; communication was extensive, and Costa Rican Indians were certainly aware of communities to the north. Why did they not think of their neighbors as markets to exploit? This begins to raise some fundamental questions of worldview.

The West, Greed, and the Will to Empire

We are considering, then, the social implications of intimately organized communities versus mass society, and the different kinds of social policies that emerge from each. Destructive social policies have emerged from mass-society governments (i.e., states), while life-sustaining and respectful policies emerge from more intimately organized societies (nations). The origins of this push toward larger and larger forms of social organization can be traced to the judeo-christian history as it evolved in the West, among catholics and protestant denominations. It is critical to review some of this history in order to see how it influences modern social policies such as sustainable development.

Daly and Cobb argue that (western) economic theory "builds on the propensity of individuals to act so as to optimize their own interests."[63] Its origins, they suggest, are in Reformation theological thinking about the fallen state of human beings. The corollary of this theological notion results in suspicion toward any human claim to "genuinely other-regarding action," at least in euro-protestant cultures. The birth of european economic theory, then, involved a macabre reversal:

> Modern economic theory originated and developed in the context of Calvinism. Both were bids for personal freedom against the interference of earthly authority. They based their bids on the conviction that beyond a very narrow sphere, motives of self-

interest are overwhelmingly dominant [in human nature]. Economic theory differed from Calvinism only in celebrating as rational what Calvinists confessed as sinful.[64]

While Daly and Cobb find that the catholic tradition was relatively more open to the possibility of other-regarding action, Robert Williams traces the West's will to empire and need to dominate to papal aspirations and canon law debate around the issue of *infidel dominium* during and between the reigns of Innocent III and Innocent IV, long before the Reformation.[65] The impact of these historical developments can be seen in the resulting prevalent western worldviews that Williams describes as an intolerance of normative divergence and the insistence that the conquest be made decisive in every case. These are essentially cultural values that demand conformity to a particular judeo-christian theological vision of the world, and they have become so ingrained in western thought that they invade and ultimately determine even so-called progressive social policies such as development or sustainable development.

The concern that all human beings be brought to one standard of living that is considered "just" and "humane" in fact becomes the coercion of diverse cultures into conformity with western priorities. In addition to destroying the fragile webs that weave together distinct cultures, this serves the purpose of reinforcing for the western system that its conquest of the world has again prevailed. Gayatri Chakravorty Spivak offers the blunt assessment that "sustainable development" is essential to the discourse of "the great narrative of development" that is funded and coordinated primarily by the World Bank. She continues, "The general ideology of global development is racist paternalism . . . ; its general economics capital-intensive investment; its broad politics the silencing of resistance and of the subaltern as the rhetoric of their protest is constantly appropriated."[66] This is an ongoing process set in motion, as Williams documents, by both catholic and protestant doctrine and practice.

Thus, we must begin to acknowledge that the confluence of christianity and european cultural traditions has indeed functioned over the past half of a millennium to create a world system that is threatening on a global scale. Both modern state forms of political governance and their variations derive from the same cultural, intellectual, and theological base. Both capitalism and marxism are deeply rooted in the spiritual and theological imagination of the West. While marxism may have tried to break the hold of individualism, it is wholly consistent with western temporality. Both capitalism and marxism are wholly developmental in their economic and political commitments and, as such, are antithetical to cultures rooted in harmony and balance.[67]

There are voices in the United States today aggressively reacting to what they call the "bashing" of western culture and traditions. Yet the evidence is relatively clear that the West—as a hegemonic cultural, economic, and social system—does indeed have its flaws, and it can be argued persuasively that its most serious flaws appear to be fatal, both to itself at a moral and spiritual level and to the whole of the world at political and environmental levels.

Certainly this situation is not unique. Precedents can be found in the history of the empires of Assyria and Babylon, Greece and Rome, each of which collapsed as it fell in on itself. What is unique to the contemporary crisis is that today's western empire is a *network* of mass-consumption societies with technologies efficient enough to destroy the world. The Davidic Empire of the Old Testament was perhaps as destructive as the other ancient empires. But David's modern manifestation as israeli Zionism presents a much more intense problem simply because Israel is part of the european-american politics of domination. Empire has become an effectively globalized "machine" comprising and represented by an international membership. It is characterized by the strength of influence with which it readily subverts the sovereignty of individual states as it manifests its primary weapons of moral, military, and juridical intervention. Hardt and Negri observe the fundamental role of "christian moral theology" and "sin" in the western imperial project as being similar to Daly's and Cobb's indictment of Reformation theology as essential in the origin of european economic theory.[68]

Indigenous Failures?

There is a lingering self-defense among many in the neoconservative, Rush-Limbaugh-dittohead set that other peoples have also abused the natural world—they just lacked the resources and technology to do it as exhaustively as europeans and americans have done.[69] A corollary defense is often argued that some earlier American Indian cultures actually met their demise because they "overstepped environmental limits." The presbyterian "Sustainability-Development Debate" makes this assertion in regard to the ancient peoples who left behind the unoccupied ruins in the U.S. Southwest that are usually called "Anasazi."[70]

This is simply not necessarily so in either case. Without unduly romanticizing American Indian communities, either past or present, it is important to recognize the significant differences between the cultural values of euro-western peoples and other state-oriented peoples, on the one hand, and those of Native American and other indigenous peoples on the other. Creativity in this moment of world crisis seems to demand openness and perspicuity here especially.

First, only White, euro-american scholarship has decided that, for instance, the Anasazi peoples met some perceived destruction because they overstepped environmental limits. Many Pueblos and Hopis, to the contrary, claim Anasazi culture as their own, meaning that the Anasazis were not destroyed but only underwent a change. That a people may make decisive changes in their way of life, moving from mesa tops or canyon floors into cliff dwellings and then moving at a later date into a different yet similar type of structure, is part of a natural response to the environment. Suffice it to say here that other explanations are just as reasonable, or perhaps even more reasonable, than those offered by White scholars who have a demonstrably vested self-interest in not embarrassing the structures of power that empower themselves.[71]

Second, there were and are cultures that took their natural world environment seriously and attempted to live in balance with the created whole around them in ways that helped them not overstep environmental limits. Unlike the West's consistent experience of alienation from the natural world,[72] these cultures of indigenous peoples consistently experienced themselves as part of that created whole, in relationship with everything else in the world. They saw and see themselves as having responsibilities, just as every other creature has particular responsibilities, for maintaining the balance of creation in an ongoing process. This is ultimately the spiritual rationale for annual ceremonies like the Sun Dance or Green Corn Dance.[73]

Historically, Lakota peoples planted cottonwoods and willows in their tipi rings and campfire sites as they broke camp to move on, thus beginning the process of reclaiming the land that humans had necessarily trampled through habitation and encampment. Modern Lakota people remember this community habit today through the continued passing on of oral tradition.[74]

Brazilian rain forest peoples, we now know more and more, had a unique relationship to the forest in which they moved away from a cleared area after farming it to a point of reduced return, allowing the clearing to be reclaimed as jungle. The group would then move to clear a new area for a new cycle of production. The whole process was and is relatively sophisticated and functioned in harmony with the integrity of the jungle itself. So extensive was their movement that some scholars are now suggesting that there is actually very little of what might rightly be called "virgin forest" in what had been considered the "untamed" wilds of the jungle.

This description is more than just a coincidence or, worse, some romanticized falsification of native memory. Rather, I am insisting that there are peoples in the world who live with an acute and cultivated awareness of their intimate participation in the natural world as part of an intricate whole. For indigenous peoples, this means that when they are presented with the concept of development, it is *sense-less*. Most significantly, it is important to realize that this worldview is the result of self-conscious effort on the part of traditional American Indian national communities and is rooted first of all in the mythology and theology of the people.

Transformation of the World System in Mythology and Theology

I want to push for a new vision of the world, a radical re-imaging of reality. And as I indicated in the beginning of this essay, this process is in some American Indian traditional circles a process of dreaming a new future. The transformation must begin with a theological shift away from the individual toward a theology that founds and sustains a community existence. The salvation of the communal whole (that is, the world) demands a theology that treats the community as a whole and avoids unnecessary fracturing of the community into individual actors. We should now be about the task of empowering communities *as* communities, rather than as individual actors in a world system geared toward personal fulfillment only.

A second theological shift—toward the priority of spatiality in our discourse and self-imaging and away from temporality—will generate a community imagination of being a part of an even greater whole. Only when our theologies and our spiritual imaginations begin to take seriously the space of our existence and even prioritize the space of our existence before the time of our existence, will we begin to resolve temporal issues of power and domination. A firm sense of spatiality puts us in an immediate spiritual and intellectual relationship with the whole of creation in ways that are not possible if our immediate relationship is to time and history.[75]

Whatever the shift, it is imperative that it be a transformation that affects all facets of western cosmology, epistemology, and social structuring. Mythology *has* to do, must have to do, with intellectual tradition as a whole, with the discipline and the practice of economics, with politics, with social structures every bit as much as with the narrower euro-western category of religion or the even narrower New Age category of spirituality. We must begin by imagining ourselves differently in the world.

The liberation of euro-american peoples must be rooted in confession and repentance with respect to their relationship with the native peoples of this continent. It is important, however, that these two terms be carefully distinguished. Confession is the expression of emotions of guilt; repentance is proactive behavior that follows confession and emotions of guilt. (See Acts 2:37-38, where Peter calls for repentance as a consequence of people's confession-related feelings of guilt.[76])

2

Indianness and Cultural Alterity

A couple of years ago, I chose to use the chapter that follows this one to provoke discussion at a faculty colloquium at my school.[1] The idea began with a relatively simple dinner exchange some weeks earlier at a faculty and staff christmas dinner. Two others at my table started to discuss the nature of what is a specifically american cognitional category, namely, the term *hometown*.[2] One of the faculty members insisted that he was necessarily unsure of what he should consider to be his hometown, since he had been born in one locale, moved in early childhood, and grew up largely in another. The other faculty member was equally sure that "hometown" must refer to the place where one grew up. As the whole Iliff [School of Theology] community knows by now, I never pass up a chance to demonstrate cultural alterity. I interjected myself into the conversation in order to provide a counter warrant that seemed to falsify this "commonsense" inferential proposition in a useful way. That moment, of course, was not the appropriate time for inferential disputation, but it did raise a useful and arguable concern for me that I thought all of you might find equally interesting.

The question I initially raised that evening was this: What about people who claim as their "hometown" places where they neither were born nor grew up?

The point that I want to argue is that American Indian individuals clearly identify with their communities, that is, with their social and cultural group of natal affiliation, rather than with the greater community that may surround them in a given place. In this postmodern moment of miscegenation, immigration, urbanization, and diasporaization, this means that a growing plurality of Indians live in urban centers around the continent that are some distance from their ancestral lands and national communities.[3] Indeed, the parents in urban Indian families may have grown up on "the rez," but increasingly children in these families, even adult children today, grew up in the city. Yet, until very recently (say, the last ten years or so), whenever an Indian person in the city is asked, "Where are you from?" the answer was almost always provided in terms of the individual's national community, that is, by naming the person's home reservation and/or providing one of the common modern names of the nation from which the person derives.

Take the following dialogue as an example:

> "So, where are you from?"
> "I'm from Pine Ridge."
> "Oh yeah? I've been to Pine Ridge. What community?"
> "Well, my dad's folk are from Wanblee, and my mother is from Ring Thunder over on the Rosebud Reservation."
> "And where did you grow up?"
> "Oh, I was born and raised right here in Denver! Went to GW High School and Metro State."

Nevertheless, the person is "from Pine Ridge." It is crucial to note in this dialogue that there is absolutely no consideration for calling Denver the person's hometown.

What this means, in brief, is that Indian persons today, living in the city, are extremely likely to name as their hometown a place where they neither were born nor grew up. I am *ni-u-ko"ska wa-zha-zha* (Osage). Where am I from? I'm from Pawhuska, Oklahoma. No, I was born somewhere else. No, I did not grow up there. It does not matter. I am from Pawhuska. It is the one place in the world where I know I will get fed and housed when I arrive. And if not in Pawhuska, then in Hominy or Grey Horse or Nilagani, all on the Osage and within twenty miles of Pawhuska, the Agency town. This area, the Osage Reservation, is where I know I have friends and family in abundance. No one there will be too busy to see me. I can knock on doors unannounced and invite myself in—even if I have been away for a couple of years.

All of this, of course, has much to do with the religious identity of Indian peoples these days, since religious identity can involve a complex that includes ancestry, culture, worldview, social location, personal history, etc., as well as personal choices. Personal choice, however, is not nearly as prominent a feature in Indian religious identity as it has been in american religious voluntarism. While denominational shifts and even religious choices can be made fairly easily in the broader american culture, changing one's tribe of affiliation is impossible. To this extent, at least, Indian religious identity begins at the level of modality rather than sodality, with birth, ancestry, and culture. Choices of sodality can happen later in life, but always within existing structures of modality. Thus, an Osage man might be initiated into the i^n-lo^n-$shka$ as a sodal organization, but the initiation requires a public naming of the person's clan (modal affiliation) and personal clan name. One is born into a clan as an aspect of modal organization. Thus one's place in the modal structure of the community is established by parentage and cannot be altered for reasons of personal preference. Likewise, an Osage could not suddenly decide to abandon the tribe and assume a new identity as a member of the Pawnee tribe—though God only knows why anyone would want to do so anyway (with apologies to my Pawnee friends for this kind of public teasing).

One remaining problem that must yet be addressed is what happens in the future, now not too distant, when spatial distance from "home" combined with miscegenation and the persistent intrusion of what Emanuel Wallerstein calls the emerging global culture—an increasingly universal culture of consumerist capitalism—all function to reshape and radically change Indian culture. That analysis will have to wait for another occasion.

Before we move into a more technical discussion of Indian identity, it might be useful to pay attention briefly to another, related contemporary (postmodern?) phenomenon. What follows is a very short open letter that I prepared as a response to the umpteenth inquiry I received from someone trying to recover a lost Indian heritage. It will actually help to put the chapter that follows, a more substantial piece concerning identity, into clearer perspective.

Lost Bloods: Biological Claims to Indianness in the Postcolonial Conquest

It happens all too often in this "postcolonial" moment—not only to me, but to many Indian persons in positions of some public exposure. It has suddenly become fashionable, and even economically advantageous in a perverse way that fails to account for Indian poverty, to make some claim to having Indian blood. There is a steady stream these days of euro-americans who have only some dim memory or even a newly discovered biological connection with some Indian tribe or another. Over the years, the most common tribe designated has been "Cherokee," a trait that has caused many a non-Cherokee to chuckle and refer to "Cherokee Sixty-Fourths" as some newly identified tribe—along with the Winnabingos. Iroquois is another common tribal identity claim—even though there is not and never has been a tribe by that name. Lakota has become increasingly common as Lakota spirituality has been co-opted on the New Age commodity market as the most accessible and perceptibly exotic Native culture in North America of the day.

While many of these claims to biological Indian heritage are wholly fictitious, a great many others are quite genuine, if relatively empty of any connective meaning. Most often persons with genuine biological claims no longer have any idea to which Indian community they have a biological connection. The family only remembers that there was Indian blood back a few generations. The question is, Are these persons Indian? Others do have a family memory of a generations-earlier tribal connection, but they have lost all cultural sense of being Indian because the culture has not been lived for all of those interceding generations.

The following is an actual reply I sent to one of these "lost-bloods" who asked for some help in discovering her Indian heritage.

Dear Friend:

As you are probably already aware, the situation you describe is one that is all too familiar in North America today. I would guess that some 30 percent of North Americans today have some degree of Indian blood tucked away in their biological heritage somewhere. Unfortunately, this has accomplished little to help American Indian peoples politically or socially. In fact, it often becomes problematic as people decide at some late (genealogical) date that they would like to opt back into the Indian community from which their ancestors had extricated them some generations before. I have written a paper [included in this volume as chapter 3] dealing with the complex issues of American Indian identity, which I hope will clarify some things for you that I will not take the time to address here.

I apologize for imposing such a lengthy answer to the seemingly simple inquiry you e-mailed to me. The problem, however, is quite complex, embedded in five hundred years of euro-western colonialism and the ongoing relationship between colonizer and colonized (see Albert Memmi; also Fanon, *Black Skin; White Masks*). So while I beg your indulgence, I insist that it is the commonness of your situation that seems to entreat such a response on my part. I hasten to add that this is a difficult issue—both intellectually and emotionally—for me to address, because it requires me to say some hard things to you and others in your situation. Please forgive anything that might seem to be an overstatement or that might seem rudely targeted.

I am afraid that I do not have much encouragement for you. Please remember that I am speaking out of the pain and struggle of the Indian community. I speak as an Indian community activist who is deeply involved in the ongoing process of community healing and development and whose first commitment is to the well-being of the Indian community (meaning both urban community and every Indian national community). I want to affirm your biological heritage and historic connection with Indian people, yet there are some terrible pitfalls that could end up consuming both of us—in different ways. Hurting yourself and/or further hurting existing Indian communities would be an unfortunate result. I do conclude with some suggestions for how you and others in your situation might learn to live with and live out of a double heritage that includes a thoroughly assimilated White cultural response to the world and knowledge of some part-Indian biological heritage.

So, it is with some reluctance that I am forced to suggest to all persons in situations similar to yours something like the following. Some of these things identify problems that are barriers that will be difficult or impossible to overcome. Others identify pitfalls that can be avoided with some self-conscious attention and care.

1. I can surely understand your emotional attachment to the discovery of a long-lost biological connection with American Indian people. Unfortunately, the cultural competency aspects of the connection have been lost long ago and replaced by the dominant cultural responses and values of North American White (or Black or Chicano) society and its cultural responses and values. Changing one's culture of attachment is nearly impossible. This is because culture involves habitual behavioral responses to the world, the vast majority of which are not conscious at the surface level in any way but are automatic and nonreflective actions and behaviors. Many of these behaviors can be linked to particular sets of values that are foundational for a society, but they are not thought through anew each time one has to act or do something. It might be something as simple and everyday as tying a shoelace. Which shoe do you tie first? It may depend, for an Indian person, on one's clan or, especially in the case of Osages, on one's moiety. For Osages, in the traditional village context where the village is divided into *tzi sho* and *hunka* divisions, both culture and spirituality begin with knowing and acting automatically, without forethought, which side of the body to favor in sleeping, getting dressed, and the like.[4] I guess the point I would make is that getting enrolled in some tribe, real or fictitious, is often easier

than gaining competency in the culture of an existent Indian national community.

2. Both clan membership and moiety attachment, like tribal affiliation itself, are birth assignations. That is, there is no choice involved whatsoever. One cannot choose to be of a particular clan, and changing one's clan of birth attachment is impossible except by marriage, depending on the tribal social arrangements, for either the male or the female. Yet clan membership is critically important to Indian identity in many national communities. For instance, clan membership among the Cherokee is matrilineal. That is, one's clan membership is determined by one's mother's clan. And without clan membership, one is not permitted entry into the "grounds" as a member ("grounds" here meaning the contemporary religious association that is configured around a particular piece of land, regular stomp dances, and the annual green corn ceremony). In the case of those whose Cherokee cultural attachment was severed by a Cherokee man taking a non-Cherokee woman, the recovery of clan membership is not possible, unless the Cherokee national community makes a communal, consensual, national decision to do so.

3. That raises yet another question. What constitutes the Cherokee Nation today? I would refer you again to the *Encyclopedia* (see note 4). See the entry "Cherokee" (105–8) written by Duane H. King (Cherokee). Essentially, there are two parts of the nation: the Eastern Band and the Cherokee Nation of Oklahoma, although the United Band of Keetoowahs, also federally recognized and a culturally competent community in Oklahoma, disputes the governance of the Cherokee Nation of Oklahoma. These three entities are the continuing, culturally competent, and politically and socially intact manifestations of the ancient Cherokee Nation. By culturally competent here, I mean the traditional culture continues to be lived in some consistent trajectory of development from the ancient national community's aboriginal existence. *Cultural competency* is a term I created in the chapter on identity [chapter 3] to help us come a little closer to understanding what *Indian* means in this postmodern and so-called postcolonial world of confusion and uncertainty. King goes on to acknowledge that some "fifty other organizations in at least twelve states claim Cherokee descent." But remember my point that claiming Cherokee descent (even legitimate descent) is quite different from "being" Cherokee in any national, cultural, or political sense. The point of my identity essay is that blood alone does not

make for Indian identity. In fact, my essay argues, culture is a much more important indicator.

4. One of the problems associated with "lost-bloods" who are discovering both that they have a little Indian biological heritage and that it is more and more acceptable to be Indian today, even desirable in some sense, is that many are making claims on Indian identity in ways that are economically advantageous to that particular neophyte but economically and socially disadvantageous for existing culturally competent communities. For example, a great many law schools today have set aside moneys, admissions, and scholarships for Indian students. Yet when Indian community activists or Indian lawyers—that is, culturally competent Indian lawyers—visit these schools, we have trouble finding any Indians at all! Typically, the twelve or fifteen students who may have gained admission to Colorado University Boulder Law School, or any other law school, as American Indians in any given year have no claim other than (distant) biological heritage to Indian identity. They have, nevertheless, used that heritage for individual economic advantage—an obvious and clear violation of Indian cultural value systems for anyone with more than a cursory understanding, in any case. For the most part, these students have no intention of even trying to become active in any actual Indian community. Mere economics and educational privilege is at stake. For others, being Indian is equally economic at base but becomes a career choice. Being publicly identified as an Indian, for instance, can lead to advantageous hiring—in the church, in the private sector sometimes, or in some level of government service. In any case, like law school students, these people presume on biological heritage in order to take the place of an actual (culturally competent) Indian person who comes out of an already economically and educationally disadvantaged social sector. In many protestant churches, for instance, the judicatory administrative process will often decide to hire one of these lost-bloods to serve in ministry to an Indian community simply because their cultural responses are much more compatible with the culture of the administrator. The net result for the Indian community is that they simply have another White missionary minister (culturally speaking). Yet the church thinks it has done something special because the person had claimed and continues to claim status as an Indian and may even have adopted a fancy Indian-sounding name.

5. One key contributing factor to the creation of lost-blood status was the economic advantage generations back of *not* being Indian. Unfortunately, those families who have historically denied their Indian

heritage have already benefited economically from that choice made by a great-grandparent a couple of generations ago. Now having assimilated, through no direct choice of their own, many persons want to do that which is nearly impossible. But another factor must be thrown into the mix. That is something I have already referenced just above, namely, the continuing postcolonial poverty and disruption of Indian communities. All too often, the community's experience of prodigal lost-bloods' attempts to return home has been that these persons fail to understand the severe poverty and dysfunction of the contemporary Indian community and have even less real long-term interest in participating in the healing process. Or they come at the problem with solutions that they would impose from their own cultural perspective. Usually, they come into the community with a much romanticized idea of what being Indian is all about. Moreover, they come often with already established lives outside of the Indian community and have no problem going back to that life in between visits in the Indian community. Indian persons do not have that luxury. We necessarily live life within the community each day and each part of every day. We cannot go home at night, that is, leave the community for some non-Indian, more comfortable refuge.

6. Of course, there is a constant problem, mentioned in my chapter about identity, that must also be clearly acknowledged and understood. This has to do with the deeply embedded differences of Indian culture and non-Indian culture, particularly euro-american culture, and how these differences will surface in any moment of cultural interaction. The last five hundred years of colonial conquest have significantly affected euro-american culture, just as they have affected Indian cultures. The habitual behavioral responses of euro-american persons are generally (and I realize that all generalizations fail to some degree every test of absolutism) in keeping with the ongoing sense of colonial responsibility toward the colonized "other." The clear and overwhelming tendency of lost-bloods, even those who may be full-bloods biologically but have been raised outside of the community (for example, because of adoption as babies—again not of their choice), is to come into the Indian community with cultural responses that are entirely too directive. They come at this newly discovered set of Indian community problems with problem-solving skills finely honed in another world and with solutions in mind that, again, might be naturally effective in that other world but are inappropriate impositions in an Indian community.

Well, I think I have written enough for now, at least enough to either excite your keen interest in a significant problem, or to have deeply and possibly irrevocably offended you. Obviously, I hope for the first and not the latter. In the final analysis, I do hope that what I have written is helpful.

In the chapter that follows, I begin to address the incredibly difficult and complex question of contemporary Indian identity.[5]

3

American Indian Religious Identity and Advanced Colonial Malignancy

Turning inside out the insistence of missionaries of a scant generation ago, a radical American Indian activist instructed a young christian Indian on a critical issue of Indian identity and religious affiliation: "You have to choose. You are either Indian or christian. You can't be both!" At the same time, Indian identity is being challenged on several other "postcolonial" fronts. A lasting result of five hundred years of colonialism and conquest, of intentional and persistent church and colonial government policy, is the continued dilution of Indian blood, a phenomenon referred to as "mixed blood," which has infused Indian communities with colonial religion and colonial culture in general. The contemporary result is a confusing plethora of questions. Who is Indian today? How can we validate claims to "tribal" blood? Can one be "Indian" and "christian"? Indeed, can one be "Indian" and "capitalist"? Or, for that matter, can one be both Indian and american? Who is a member of any Indian national community ("tribe")? Does one have to be a "member" of a "tribe" in order to be Indian? How is membership determined, and who determines it? And who can legitimately participate in or perform "tribal" ceremonial acts? This last question is a way of asking a harsher question: When does being Indian become no more than a maudlin postmodern act of ludic simulation?[1]

Indian identity questions are very complex and thoroughly infused with the lasting residuals of colonial domination. The "missionaries" (both religious and secular/civil) put considerable energies into separating Indian peoples from their cultures and, not least of all, from that particular cultural aspect of their community lives that euro-americans have called "religion."

The nineteenth-century slogan devised by R. H. Pratt, the founder of Carlisle Indian School, summed it up nicely: "Kill the Indian . . . and save the man." Since "kill the Indian" was a clear metaphoric reference to Indian culture and values—specifically religious values and cultural practices—the slogan affirmed what was the latest effort to force the social and cultural transformation of Indian persons, particularly children, from Indian into euro-american clones.[2] Until a generation ago, mainline missionaries were quick to insist that we Indians had to choose between the individual salvation of our souls (christian conversion) and Indian community ceremonial responsibilities (cultural integrity). Modern "evangelicals" tend, of course, to continue the same insistence today. It is an act of resistance for some contemporary Indian spiritual leaders to insist today that one must choose between christianity and being Indian, just at the moment when the mainline churches have begun to make accommodations to Indian culture and spirituality.

This discussion only begins to unveil the complexity of the contemporary Indian experience.[3] This chapter will explore some of that complexity in attempting to shed light on some of these questions, such as: Who is Indian? What are Indian religious traditions and identity? And how will all of this affect public policy in the new millennium? While there is no satisfying essentialist definition for Indian identity, there are enough "family resemblances" to help sort out some of the complexity.

The U.S. government and its (quasi) private citizen zealots such as Pratt have long pursued the same practical ends as the missionaries. Namely, a religious sort of conversion to euro-american culture, along with the creation of new legal fictions and governmental policies to encourage and coerce the conversion of Indian peoples,[4] was seen as the only course, short of extermination, for allowing the safe and sure appropriation of Indian lands and resources.[5] To this extent, mainline religious missionaries were (and still are today) in deep collusion with their secular counterparts,[6] and in the late nineteenth century, the two came together most openly and explicitly in an annual meeting under the euphemism "Friends of the Indian."[7] Together, church and state created numerous devices and policies intentionally designed to separate Indian people from their cultures and their religious traditions and to encourage a mixing of bloods to weed out the last remnants of Indianness.

This strategy to eradicate Indianness from Indian communities was, it must be remembered, the liberal alternative. After the U.S. civil war, voices across the country, especially in the west, were crying for outright extermination of Indians. In a real sense, however, this liberal policy was still extermination, even if the extermination goal was more implicit and covert, not to say more satisfying to christian moral qualms. More to the point, the extermination of

Indian peoples continues to this day as the implicit policy of the U.S. government. This has been readily apparent during the past half century in U.S. policies of termination,[8] relocation,[9] female sterilization,[10] economic co-optation, the continuing compromises of Indian national sovereignties (for example, in anti-Indian gaming measures), etc. The continuing attempts of churches to replace community ceremonial commitments with their own denominational hegemony, even when they liberally include elements from the cultural traditions of their victims, represents the continued collaboration of churches with the subtle "extermination" objectives of the U.S. government.[11]

Colonizer Privilege and Legal Signifiers

The first concern has to do with asking who is qualified (i.e., privileged) to determine Indian identity. In terms of U.S. government policy, the colonial power has regularly assumed the prerogative of naming the colonial other. Others among the colonizer class have regularly presumed a similar colonial prerogative, most notably by churches, in terms of the sorts of Indian persons that colonizer institutions choose to empower as comprador elites.[12] A careful selection of compradors (e.g., "tribal" officials, lay evangelists, catechists, and delegates) can ensure continued dominance of the colonized, whether by church or state.

Ngugi wa Thiong'o contends that every day, the colonizer unleashes the most powerful weapon available against the "collective defiance" of the colonized people; he calls this weapon the "culture bomb."[13] The effect of the culture bomb is to eradicate the beliefs, traditions, names, and all other aspects of identity and self-reliance held by the people. As a response to the despondency and despair of the wasteland caused by the culture bomb, "imperialism presents itself as the cure and demands that the dependent sing hymns of praise with the constant refrain: 'Theft is Holy.'"[14] Rigorous self-reflection on the part of colonizer institutions, whether governmental or church, is necessary before the colonizer will be able to surrender its presumed privilege to determine the legitimacy of Indian identity.

Charles Long, in *Significations*, analyzed the structural inability of many marginalized (racialized) communities to signify themselves and the corresponding tendency of those representing the power center of society to freely signify the marginalized.[15] Rather, marginalized racial-ethnic communities consistently live in a world where we are signified by others, especially by a dominant systemic whole whose power often depends on their ability to signify dominated population sectors. American Indians (south as well as north)

have been in such a signified relationship with the colonizers for half a millennium. Thus, asking how one identifies Indian qua Indian must begin with
identifying the colonial need for any such identification. The stakes are, of
course, colonial control of the colonized in order to facilitate the complete
colonial acquisition of the territories and resources of the colonized. Colonial
bureaucracy provided a couple of strategies, introducing blood quantum
measurements and legal tribal enrollment. Eventually, of course, the dependency of the colonized on the colonizer—a successful part of the colonizer
strategy—entered the picture and generated an additional complexity with
regard to Indian identity.

Given the undeniable existence of legal treaty documents (U.S. Constitu-
tion, Article VI, where treaties are identified as the "highest law of the land"),
the U.S. government found itself in the later part of the nineteenth century
with a constant pecuniary obligation to tribes. Having finally taken Indian
lands and resources by violence or by mendacity and political manipulation,
reducing that pecuniary obligation became an attractive expedience. For a
country with some collective "Enlightenment" sense of self-righteousness,
only a couple of possibilities other than the simple and overt extermination of
Indian peoples seemed to exist for reducing rent payments. One was to somehow negotiate a reduction in the numbers of those legally included as members of tribal nations. The other involved creating laws and policies that might
reasonably lead to a decline in the cultural integrity of Indian people and,
thus, reduce their recognizability as culturally different. One way to manipu-
late the size of these communities toward a continued decline in numbers was
to encourage intermarriage. Another was to separate Indian children from
their families in government- and church-run boarding schools.

Eventually a new strategy emerged to deny recognition as Indian to those
offspring of mixed marriages who had less than a specified percentage of blood
heritage in their national community. Hence, *blood quantum* measurements
became a favorite U.S. colonial mechanism for identifying Indian people in
such a way as to ensure the exclusion of a growing number of colonized community members from official legal identification.[16] Today, every enrolled
member of a "tribe" is issued a "Certificate of Degree of Indian Blood," or a
CDIB card. The existence and employment of this pernicious tool of discrimination and domination should never be mentioned without also noting that
only Nazi Germany and apartheid South Africa have engaged in such a practice of overt official signifying.[17] The blood quantum rules imposed historically
on "tribal" governments most often still pertain today. One must have a minimum of one-quarter blood heritage of a specific "tribe" to qualify as a member.
Blood quantum, then, is the usual determiner applied by the federal govern-

ment to determine Indianness. With the ever-increasing rate of intermarriage, even intermarriage between different Indian communities ("tribes"), the government can count on an intentional diminishing and eventual elimination of Indian "tribes."

It may be helpful to see a few statistics in order to gain a sense of the imminence of this ongoing project of "diminishing" the number of "status" Indians. The 1990 U.S. Census reported nearly 1.9 million persons self-identified as American Indians, but only 746,128 were actually enrolled in a U.S. recognized tribe. Of even greater significance is the work of researchers such as Joanne Nagel and C. Matthew Snipp, analyst and demographer respectively, and native scholar Jack D. Forbes, whose conclusions allow for a reasonable working estimate of the number of "ethnic Indians" to be from 7 million upwards to 15 million persons.[18]

Challenging the quarter-blood rule (as many "tribes" have) then raises another set of questions: How high a blood quantum is necessary before one can be reasonably considered Indian? Should this blood quantum be necessarily of a single national community? At what point should someone be excluded from the community because of declining blood quantum? And who should be authorized to officially engage in such splitting of hairs? The truth seems to be that the colonizer's state apparatus has much invested in limiting the number of people legally or officially signified as "Indian." The irresolvable paradox is, then, that the colonizer created the problems we experience with regard to Indian identity, and then the colonizer moved continually to solve the very problems they themselves created. Needless to say, the colonizer state bureaucracy always proposes solutions that ultimately work to the state's own benefit.[19]

Enrollment is one of those bureaucratic processes that characterize european "modernity" and, in this case, signifies legal membership in a "tribe." The word *tribe* has been sufficiently critiqued by Churchill in terms of its derivation from zoology and the taxonomic need to distinguish animals.[20] "Tribes" are, first of all, relatively artificial constructs of the U.S. government, sometimes lumped together for the convenience and efficiency of the state. "Tribal government" is a configuration that is decidedly colonial in design (*à la* the 1934 Indian Reorganization Act of the U.S. Congress) and has very little to do with American Indian self-signification. Typically, members of the "tribal" council are the last people consulted on traditional cultural and religious knowledge. "Tribal" membership was initially recorded and bureaucratically maintained by U.S. government officials.

The question most often asked today is, Are you "enrolled"? Many Indian persons today are not so enrolled and have no CDIB card but are often as culturally competent as many who are officially enrolled. Some families rejected enrollment as acts of colonial resistance. Some, because of intercommunity marriages (e.g., boarding school marriages), could no longer demonstrate the requisite quarter-blood quantum of a single "tribe" to be enrolled in one of, say, six or seven tribes of one's heritage.[21] The U.S. government identifies persons as Indian on the basis of blood quantum and on the basis of "tribal" membership. Thus, access to Indian Health Service facilities, scholarships, small-business loans, and other programs will depend on enrollment status, often with the added proviso of a minimum blood quantum designation.

This critique of blood quantum and "tribal" enrollment makes our original question of Indian identity even more pressing and persistent. If blood quantum and "tribal" enrollment are colonial impositions created historically by the colonizer government for the convenience of and to enhance the control of the colonizer in North America, how should public policy today proceed in an anticolonial modality for the future? Who is Indian, and how will the body politic (government, churches, and civil institutions) recognize us if they cannot themselves make the official/legal determination? How will Indians signify themselves now at the end of a half-millennium of colonial conquest and control? For example, how will entitlements—i.e., "treaty" entitlements—be distributed by the federal government (or by other institutions, such as churches and universities)? These "entitlements" would include funding set-asides for Indian communities, projects, or programs; scholarships targeted for Indian individuals; affirmative-action jobs; health care; and the like. The imposition of blood quantum designations and bureaucratic "tribal" enrollment regulations continue the historic colonial relationships and are clear violations of Indian sovereignty. On the other hand, there ought logically to be some way to answer these questions.

If blood quantum and enrollment are not adequate or historically appropriate means for determining Indianness, then the other logical determinant seems to be cultural adherence, or cultural competency. Notice that there is no notion of cultural competency currently involved in public policy identification of Indianness. Yet in Indian communities,[22] cultural competency is far more important than blood quantum or enrollment. Traditionally, the only question in an Indian community has been whether a person belongs to the community, whether they are a significant, participating part of the national community, and not whether they have some arbitrarily predetermined percentage of national community blood. On the other hand, belonging never had to do with some legal paperwork that identified the person as such. Rather, the community already knew, immediately knew, whether someone was a participant in community life or not. Even today, the real question of whether one is full blood or mixed has to do with cultural competency in daily life activities within the community.

Cultural Competency, Including Religious Practice

A number of specific tests might be applied in order to indicate Indian cultural competency. They may seem somewhat intangible to euro-americans, but members of the American Indian community, whether reservation based or urban, usually have little trouble in recognizing one another as members of their community.

The first of these tests would ask whether the individual is a regular and natural participant in some Indian community—again, for example, either reservation or urban. It is nearly impossible to maintain cultural competency when one lives outside of the community, since cultural behavior habits are formed and constantly reinforced only in community.

Also, when individuals come into the community and make claims to Indian heritage, people will regularly ask who their relatives are. As Deloria suggested a quarter of a century ago, there are no Indians who do not know their relatives.[23] This knowing, of course, must include knowing what community one is attached to, culturally as well as in terms of bloodline. Thus, it is an everyday occurrence when Indian persons meet to ask, "Where are you from?" The correct answer is never the city where one might live, but rather the reservation community of one's heritage.

The third test is related to knowing one's relatives and has to do with connection to the land, something I will discuss more directly later in the chapter. Here the concern has to do with ongoing relationships with the "home" community. How is the individual connected to her or his reservation community? Does the person return "home" at regular intervals? Is the person in relationship with "elders" and relatives "back home"? These are highly desirable aspects of cultural competency.

Fourth, the community will always weigh the cultural integrity of the individual, with respect to the national community to which that person claims connection. There is something wrong in a situation where someone claims some vague attachment to one community yet practices a ceremonial life of another community as a way of living out one's Indianness. Since Indian communities are modal social organizations as opposed to sodalities, national ("tribal") affiliation is never a matter of choice but of birth. Likewise, ceremonial participation/affiliation is always community specific, with the actual ceremonial structures varying sometimes radically from national community to national community. For someone claiming Choctaw heritage, for instance, participating in a Lakota Sun Dance can never be a sufficient level of participation by itself to clarify cultural competency.

These four tests of cultural competency are eventually rooted in some basic cultural norms that are particular to all Indian peoples. Indeed, these cultural foundations seem to function similarly for indigenous peoples in other places around the globe and differentiate the indigenous from other cultures that surround them. At the level of the deep structure of community existence, there are four fundamental cultural differences between Indian people and the cultures that derive from european traditions. These differences set American Indian cultures (including religious traditions, politics, etc.) distinctly apart from euro-american cultures and religions. They are, briefly noted, spatiality as a general frame of reference, attachment to particular lands or territory in particular, the priority of community over the personal (or "individual"), and a consistent notion of the interrelatedness of humans and the rest of creation.

Looking at these cultural competencies in greater detail, indigenous traditions are spatially based rather than temporally based. The euro-western world's two-thousand-year history is characterized by a trajectory that has shifted decidedly away from any rootedness in spatiality toward an ever-increasing awareness of temporality. Whether cloaked in its capitalist or socialist (marxist?[24]) guise, history and temporality reign supreme in the Euro-west, where time is money.[25] On the other hand, Native American spirituality, values, social and political structures, and even ethics are rooted not in some temporal notion of history but in spatiality. This is perhaps the most dramatic—and largely unnoticed—cultural difference between Native American thought processes and the western intellectual tradition. The western intellectual tradition is firmly rooted in the priority of temporal metaphors and thought processes. Native Americans think inherently spatially and not temporally.[26] The question is not whether time or space is missing in one culture or the other, but which metaphoric base functions as the normative base, and which is subordinate. Of course Native Americans have a temporal awareness, but it is subordinate to our sense of spatiality. Likewise, the western tradition has a spatial awareness, but that lacks the priority of the temporal. Hence, progress, history, development, evolution, and process become key notions that invade all academic discourse in the West, from science and economics to philosophy and theology. History, thus, becomes the quintessential western intellectual device and gives rise to structures of cognition and modes of discourse that pay dutiful homage to temporality.[27]

Second, American Indian indigenous cultures are communitarian by nature and do not share the Euro-west's capitulation to the importance of the individual over against community.[28] Thus, for instance, spiritual involvement in the ceremonial life of a community is typically engaged in "for the sake of the people," and not for the sake of the individual's self-enhancement. This alone sets Indian cultures and spirituality radically apart from New Age seekers and the whole european and euro-american genre of self-improvement.

Third, in the indigenous world, there is a firmly established notion of the interrelatedness of the entire created/natural world. This sense of interrelatedness means that there is a much larger community whole than the clan or village or band, and furthermore has enormous import for understanding the religious traditions of these peoples. Yet this larger community is not the modern state, but rather consists of animals (four-leggeds), birds, and all the living, moving things (including rocks, hills, trees, and rivers), along with all the other sorts of two-leggeds (humans) in the world. Indian cultures are acutely aware of being a part of creation, rather than being somehow apart from creation with some freedom to consume it at will.

Finally, spatiality, a community-centered sense, and the notion of interrelatedness lend themselves to the fourth categorical difference between these indigenous cultures and the West. In native North America, indigenous peoples find their primary attachments in terms of land and territory. Individual ownership, even group ownership, of land is a foreign concept to Indian peoples. Rather, there is a firm sense of filial attachment to particular places that comes with a responsibility to relate to the land in those places.

These four cultural identifiers are related and intertwined. If the primary metaphor of existence for Native Americans is spatial and not temporal, this goes a long way toward explaining what nearly everyone already knows, that American Indian spirituality and American Indian existence in general are deeply rooted in the land. It explains why the history of our conquest and removal from our lands was so culturally and genocidally destructive to our tribes. Perhaps the most precious gift that American Indians have to share with other peoples is our perspective on the interrelatedness of all of creation and our deep sense of relationship to the land in particular. We are all relatives: from buffaloes and eagles to trees and rocks, mountains and lakes. Just as there is no category of the inanimate, there can be no conception of anything in the created world that does not share in the sacredness infused in God's act of creation. Traditional stories relate dialogue and interaction between different animal relatives quite as if they were like us human beings. Indeed, they may have been in some earlier age. Many tribal traditions then include stories that try to account for the necessity, for the sake of the survival of one species, of violent acts, such as those perpetuated in hunting. In many of these stories, the four-leggeds and wingeds engage in long debate that concludes with a consensus to permit hunting by two-leggeds—for their good, that is, survival—but establishes certain limits that will always ensure respect for the sacredness of all life.

These characteristics manifest themselves repeatedly in the spiritual and ceremonial life of indigenous peoples in North America and among a great variety of the world's indigenous peoples.[29] So, in spite of the long-lived and ongoing colonial effort to reduce Indian difference to euro-american sameness, qualitative differences persist between Indian and euro-american.

Complications in Cultural Competency

Introducing cultural competency as an identification test does not solve all of the public policy complications. Quite to the contrary, cultural competency is itself an enigmatic category of late colonialism with its own complexities. Because of the long and intense history of colonialism, complexities arise from increasingly important questions of cultural hybridity.[30] How can we test for cultural competency when Indian individuals have been so deeply affected in such a variety of ways by the values and structures of colonialism? Some of the same problems that have already been mentioned with respect to colonial institutional policies (governmental, church, etc.) have already generated problems of cultural hybridity that make any claims to cultural competency all the more difficult. The mixing of cultures is already apparent in the context of mixed-marriage offspring. What, for example, will a child learn inherently, absorbing by familial, environmental osmosis, from parents who represent two very different cultures? Likewise, Indian people suffered culturally for a century from the forced imposition of educational structures that intentionally tried to separate Indian children from their cultures—not to mention separating them from their parents and families in boarding schools across the continent.[31] Still today, colonizer institutions (e.g., governments and churches) continue to develop policies that reward Indian persons who further distance themselves from their birth cultures and capitulate to the value system of the colonial power. This is especially apparent today in terms of the colonizer economic system of globalization, capitalism, etc.

Cultural hybridization (mixed culture) has become radically apparent as Indian demography has shifted in the past twenty years with the persistent migration of Indians away from reservations to urban centers. Beginning in 1956, encouraging American Indian emigration (with considerable duress) became an established U.S. government policy.[32] The plan was to relocate reservation families to urban centers, hoping finally to assimilate Indian people into the colonial mainstream and thus legally relieve the United States of its burdensome fiduciary responsibility toward the former landowners of the continent. Even though the policy was officially discontinued in 1970, the demographics of the Indian world have shifted, and two or three generations of Indian children have grown up away from the concentrated cultural environment of their national communities. Three very significant and foreboding trends in regard to assimilation and Indian population growth have been noted, beginning with the 1960 census figures and tracking through to the 1990 Census of the Population by the U.S. Bureau of the Census. In that period of thirty years, the urban Indian population increased by 720 percent while the rural Indian population increased by 218 percent. In a second pattern, U.S. states that historically had contained small Indian populations ("non-Indian states") registered an increase in Indian population of 114 percent, compared with a 56 percent increase in "Indian states."[33] Thus, urban Indian communities are in continual discussions these days over how to increase the cultural awareness of these Indian children born and raised in the city. It is a battle we are regularly losing as our children find their own places in the gang-infested landscape of America's cities at the beginning of this millennium—assimilated into the mainstream of America's urban communities of color and poverty.

We can even add further to this complexity by asking whether some are any longer Indian or not, and realizing that the answers to such questions are always enigmatic. Imagine a particular case of immigration, of intentional hybridization: a person born into a national community who has experienced the trauma of reservation life in such a way that she or he leaves at a very young age to seek a "better life" in the world away from the reservation. Suppose further that this person is so alienated by reservation experiences and so enamored with the White euro-american world, its culture, its values, its opportunities for advancement and individual wealth that she or he chooses to never return to the squalor of the reservation or pay attention again to anything "Indian," even in the city. Quite apart from any blood quantum consideration, the question must be raised: Is that person Indian? (Please remember that to ask the question is not to suggest an answer!)

Suppose, in another scenario, someone who has so alienated him- or herself from the national community—by engaging in inappropriate acts that threaten the integrity of the community—that she or he is too embarrassed to return for any occasion. Yet that person is still legally (officially) a member of the tribe. Is that person still Indian?

Both of these scenarios do happen with some regularity. Euro-americans can often heap praise on the Indian who has mastered the euro-american cultural effects of individual achievement, individual competition, and free-market capitalism. The religiously trained Indian who is something of a cultural expert but uses community religious knowledge as a commodity resource and takes it into the market is quite common today and very popular among New Age Whites.[34] Thus, the individual may have alienated her- or himself by engaging in "perfectly good" entrepreneurial capitalism, having discovered the great appeal these days of Indian spirituality in the outside world. Yet the home community will feel violated because of the perception that the knowledge of the person is not the person's private property to teach for a price to anyone who can afford it. Rather, they will see that knowledge as belonging to the community as a whole. In this example, we have an "Indian" person who is, in some respects, highly competent culturally—and is recognized as such by many. Yet this very person has violated the trust of the community in ways that ought to indicate profound cultural incompetency.

A further question could be raised with respect to yet another "type" of postcolonial Indian person. Suppose that this person has decided to capitulate and to adopt another culture, either the culture of the euro-american colonizer or some other subculture such as mormonism or fundamentalist christianity. All too often, this person comes back to the home community as something of an evangelist, attempting to convert others to this new culture and its patterns of behavior. In this scenario, why should the home community not consider this person an enemy of the nation who puts the cultural integrity of the whole community at risk?

The problem with such a posture is that all of us suffer some degree of hybridity. At what point will we identify hybridity as dangerous? Too many Indians have lived so long in hybrid situations that they have assumed foreign cultural traits without even being conscious of the fact. It is increasingly important to ask what the next generation will learn from the cultural hybridity of the previous generation.

Adoption, Blood, and Culture: Further Complications

In every urban Indian community, there are more-than-occasional full-bloods who surface in the community but were raised outside of the community. Perhaps they were adopted out at birth and were raised completely immersed in euro-american culture, yet they physically appear to be full-bloods. Given that their learned cultural responses to the world are euro-american and that they have zero cultural competency within the Indian community, do they have any right to claim membership? On the other hand, it was not their choice and usually not their families' choice that these infants were adopted away from their Indian community. Thus, Indian people tend to feel some obligation to attempt the reintegration of these culturally incompetent adults back into the Indian world. At the same time, this process of reintegration is incredibly difficult and not without significant risk to the entire Indian community. The danger is that, having been brought up in the euro-american world and having learned that culture and set of values at a deep and instinctive level, the candidate for reintegration can all too easily infect the Indian world with those values and cultural responses.

By the early 1970s, fully half of all Indian children were regularly being adopted out to non-Indian (White) families, replacing the boarding schools that had been the "civilizing" surrogate parents to Indian children for most of a century. In 1978 the U.S. Congress, under pressure from Indian activists, found it necessary to pass the Indian Child Welfare Act (ICWA). The act became necessary, in part, to bring the United States into compliance with the 1948 UN Genocide Convention (particularly Article IIe)[35] and to correct some of the most blatant abuses of a century-long practice of removing Indian children from their natural parents and home communities—a key part of the intentional, policy-driven effort to destroy Indian cultural competency.

There were always a variety of "rationales" for these adoptions. The modern social service agencies were largely county- or state-run institutions, and not "tribally" controlled. The standards applied to Indian families were normative standards that derived from euro-american religious identity and the corresponding notions of what healthy families ought to look like. That healthy families were presumed to share euro-american nuclear structure should not be surprising. The resultant consequence was that the predominantly White social services institutions totally failed to understand traditional American Indian family structures. When a nuclear unit within an Indian family is beset with crisis, whether short- or long-term, the family structure has a built-in safety net—namely, that aspect of Indian families that has caused colonial anthropologists to speak in terms of the "extended family." If the birth parents are unable to provide care and nurture, quite often grandparents or aunts and uncles take over those responsibilities. Yet the White social worker, with the practiced professional gaze of the colonizer judging the colonized Other, quickly confirmed the lack of compliance with dominant-culture nuclear family standards and regularly removed the children from the family, placing them instead with what seemed to them to be more suitable White adoptive or foster parents.

While the ICWA changed this situation considerably, giving "tribes" (that is, the child's ethno-national community) the first opportunity to place the child, we are still left today with thousands of mixed- and full-blood Indian adults who were raised culturally outside of the Indian world as euro-americans. Their skin may be as dark as any culturally competent full-blood, yet their cultural competency in the Indian world is as completely lacking as any White-skinned euro-american.[36] At the same time, it is important to note that, as adults, these children found that their skin color was a significant barrier against success and happiness in the racist world of late capitalist colonialism. As a result, a great many disconnected Indian adults who were raised in White adoptive families—often from infancy—attempt reintegration into an Indian community, usually in some urban environment. The difficulty is that these "Indian" persons share no habitual patterns of behavior, including values, with the community into which they seek reintegration. Given the great appeal of Indian spirituality today, many of these Indian individuals attempt that reintegration through involvement in Indian or even pseudo-Indian/New Age religious activities, which are more prevalent in cities. Thus, the complex moment of late colonial domination results in full-blood Indian persons deeply enmeshed in the make-believe world of White New Age Indian simulation.

Conversion and Capitulation: Hybrid Religion

Given culture as the important determinant, what are we to make of all our relatives who have abandoned the traditional cultural unity of spiritual practice by converting to the religion of the colonizer? Can one be christian and Indian simultaneously? This is a legitimate query. Yet, at this late stage of the colonial encounter, the legitimacy of the query could be challenged simply because so many Indian persons have capitulated to colonial religion.

Initially in the colonial experience of conquest, Indians were often physically and politically coerced into conversion.[37] Early in the enterprise of conquest and missionization, many converted out of desperation. In the face of the overwhelming power and numbers of the advancing White world, conversion was an attempt to stave off continuing disaster and to access the perceived power of Whites. In other words, conversion was sometimes an active act or attempted act of resistance, however futile. For many communities, then, conversion was a matter of survival. For some, the new religious connection became infused into the culture, molding the culture to the shape of the church. For others, the conversion was much more shallow, merely an outward appearance or surface structure. In many of these contexts, the traditional spiritual structures of the ancients actually continue to live as sort of a parallel universe to the missionary religion. The outward commitment to the mission religion allows for a layer of protection for the traditional cultural values and the ceremonial forms that accompany those values. The Pueblo communities of the Southwest are prime examples.[38]

For a great variety of reasons, then, as the colonial history of conquest unfolded, many found it useful, or practical, or necessary to convert to christianity. Today, many of us are of mixed ancestry, Indian and non-Indian, and have been brought into christianity through euro-american christian parentage. Some full-bloods made the conversion simply because they could see the privileged status of mixed-bloods in comparison to themselves. Conversion, then, was an attempt to mimic the mixed-blood experience and gain some of the advantage that White euro-americans seemed to bestow automatically on mixed-bloods.

More Complications

Those who are thin-blood by quantum measurements but are culturally well integrated into the community do not usually present an identity problem in Indian communities. Their cultural competency is not questioned by the community, except in cases where a full-blood individual uses blood quantum as a privileging mechanism in an internal power struggle within a community. Rather, these individuals' cultural identity is all too often questioned by colonizer romanticists who are disappointed by a lack of skin color and an obviously low blood quantum measurement. Of course, there is the collateral problem that colonizer individuals and institutions have scant knowledge and very few legitimate resources for qualifying Indian identity. Consequently, they are just as liable to inappropriately empower or privilege a person who claims Indian identity—whether full-blood or mixed-blood.

On the other hand, what do we do with thin-bloods who have for some generations lived outside of the national community and now, at this late date, want back in, for whatever reasons? They may have some family memory of having had an Indian ancestor (all too often, an Indian woman ancestor on their grandmother's side, perhaps even an "Indian princess," whatever that might be). They might even have some idea of the national community to which their ancestor is presumed to have belonged, although that information is usually unknown. Now that it is popular to be Indian, they are knocking at our doors (especially our ceremonial doors), claiming some relational status. Do Indian communities have any obligation to receive these long-lost relatives, now void of any bit of cultural competency, back into our midst? And to what community will we welcome them if they either have no idea what their tribal heritage actually is (some vague memory of Indianness) or claim heritage in some community far away from the place where they live or far from the Indian community to which they want to relate? After several generations of their being White, how will we suddenly teach them a whole new set of habitual responses to the world?

Unfortunately, culture—that is, habitual patterns of behavior—is very difficult to change. What happens invariably and ironically is that these "Whites," who see becoming Indian as a source of personal salvation for themselves, actually introduce the insidious and wicked virus of individualism and ego, the cornerstones of the culture of their rearing, into the Indian context. Thus, wanting to learn Indian culture, they end up introducing White culture into Indian culture as a viral contamination. All of this directly affects concerns of religious identity of Indian people, since religious concerns cannot be isolated from other cultural habits in the Indian world.

Who Can Do These Things?

With the stunning turnaround of New Age approbation of Indian spirituality, American Indian *religious* identity is made all the more treacherous, as countless "wannabes" make claims on that identity—for profit, for individual self-gratification, or even just for spite. As an increasing number of spiritual seekers make their way, invited and uninvited, into Indian community ceremonies, there is a building threat to the cultural integrity of those Indian communities. Swirling smoke from burning sage, pushed toward a participant with some large feather, preferably an eagle feather; the droning sound of a drum; perhaps even an authentic song from some (probably Lakota) Indian cultural tradition. But is it Indian?! If, and this is a sizeable *if*, the ceremony could in fact be enacted authentically, it could still only be a hollow mimicry—an act of colonizer hybridity—bereft of the tradition, life experience, and worldview where it was born, performed, and understood.

Thus, questions of Indian identity must eventually raise questions about Indian ceremonial life and the appropriateness of intercultural participation in those events. Are they Indian community events exclusively? Or can anyone play? As I explained earlier in this chapter, to be Indian is to be imbued with the cultural referent that is at one and the same time spiritual, social, political, and communal. Furthermore, no one of these constituents is viable apart from the whole. Euro-western epistemology requires everything to be categorized and thereby available for objective examination and actuation. While Indian identity is first of all "tribal," american religious identity is characterized by voluntarism—even as american culture generally is conflated with christianity. That is to say, in America—as in Europe—religious membership and participation are free choices of the participants, and making a change from one denomination to another is as simple as taking a short membership instruction course or filling out the appropriate membership forms. To the contrary, being Indian is a matter of birth. Changing one's tribe of birth is not possible; even a person's clan membership (within the tribe) is a given that cannot be changed at will. This difference in establishing religious identity makes for an interesting point of friction between Indian people and those spiritual seekers in the general american population.

Today, Indian religious traditions have been stolen and parodied by countless copycats, some of whom have gained credibility by spending a short time in actual Indian ceremonies indulging their fantasies. A couple of years ago, for example, a report arrived from the Florida American Indian Movement that a White woman calling herself "Bear" (a catchy, Indian-sounding name), having danced in a Lakota Sun Dance ceremony, had allegedly established herself in the how-to workshop business. We are told that she drew 250 people at $1,500 per person to a recent event.[39] The susceptible are quickly separated from their wallets in return for some illusion of spiritual well-being, yet Indian communities are left the poorer as misperceptions and falsified interpretations of our world are sold for profit. Thus, Indian cultural traditions, particularly those that are identified as spiritual or religious traditions, have emerged as commodities of trade in the Great American Supermarket of Fetish Spirituality.

Yet the case must be clearly stated that these outwardly appearing Indian forms (ceremonial forms) are no longer Indian in any respect once they leave the community. Rather, they are being pressed to serve the euro-american cultural needs of the individual. The surface structure still looks Indian, but the deep structure reality is far different. No longer is the well-being of a whole community the focus of the ceremonial act. Indian spirituality has become the playground, then, of the liberally minded, self-affirming contemporary colonizer. For all intents and purposes, it becomes something to dabble in, a distraction from a life that is rote, or an exotic expression of the return to nature.

It is easy to criticize Indian persons who have co-opted tribal spiritual knowledge as their own—both as personal possession and as commodity. On the other hand, non-Indians may well have an individual responsibility to say no to inappropriate invitations (i.e., almost all invitations) extended by Indian individuals to participate in intimate, ceremonial acts of Indian communities. In any case, the misappropriation of Indian spirituality by non-Indians further erodes and problematizes contemporary Indian identity.

Conclusion

In the context of contemporary colonialism, after five hundred years of political, cultural, spiritual, and emotional encroachment, the issue of American Indian identity has become incredibly complex—both for the colonized and for the colonizer. This chapter has not offered a great deal in the way of resolution; instead, it has been an attempt to explicate some of that complexity. Perhaps the one conclusion we might draw is that Indian identity is not for colonials to decide—not for contemporary colonial institutions like church or state, nor for individual non-Indian Americans. Indeed, we might go somewhat further, given the communitarian nature of Indian cultures, and argue that it is not for any individual (Indian or non-Indian) to decide, but for Indian communities to determine who is one of them and who is not.

At this late date in colonial history, we Indians are left to wonder, What is left? Who are we, culturally, religiously, politically? As a result, considerable American Indian energy is regularly invested in the question of determining who is what and what one is. The concern invades Indian politics, Indian social service activities, Indian entitlement determinations, Indian religious participation, and Indian social life in general. Moreover, questions of American Indian identity—religious, cultural, political, and social—have an enduring importance for the other americans who share this continent with it aboriginal inhabitants. They are particularly critical for the euro-americans who currently exert dominant political control over Indian national communities and over the entire continent (without addressing the globalization stratum of dominance exerted by the United States in the rest of the world). This essay has addressed the complexity of these concerns in a way that speaks to all the public institutions of the United States that affect American Indian communities, particularly governments and churches, as key actors in this continuing saga that we can now call "late-colonial malignancy."

4

American Indian Religious Traditions, Colonialism, Resistance, and Liberation
That the People May Live!

Self-mutilation. Self-torture. These were the judgments pronounced by appalled missionaries and U.S. government officials who were allowed the privilege of witnessing the Sun Dance. The ceremony is indeed brutally demanding in certain ways. Months of preparation and days of hard physical labor culminate in four days of dry fasting (no food, no liquids); dancing from dawn to dusk under a blazing sun that produces temperatures of 100 degrees or more in the confined sacred *center*; and finally offering the flesh of one's chest to be skewered and tied to a tree until dancing tears the skewers from the skin. Few people in their right mind would willingly choose to engage in such a religious act of self-abuse.

And yet, as the dancers leave the center at the end of the fourth day, tears of sadness roll down one dancer's cheeks and drip onto the wounds of the day before. The impending separation from the center, from the tree that has given its life even as the dancers sacrificed themselves, generates this bittersweet melancholy, and the dancer finds himself mumbling a prayer of commitment promising to return the following summer.

They come to dance for a great variety of reasons. Actually each Indian person has his (or increasingly, her) own discrete reasons which may or may not be shared with others. Yet, in actuality, there is only one reason to dance this ceremony. "That the people may live!" Anyone who does not understand this simple fact should stay home or at least stay out of the center, perhaps remaining under the arbor where learning can take place and where one can support those in the center. There is too much at stake. The well-being of the whole community depends on the hard spiritual work of a few who have made the commitment on behalf of the whole.

Beginning in the 1880s, in the interests of the doctrine of manifest destiny, it became U.S. government policy to outlaw specific American Indian ceremonies that were deemed dangerous impediments to the twin projects of civilizing Indian peoples and systematically relieving them of their land holdings. Christian churches in the United States contributed significantly to this cause of colonial expansion by providing on-site policing services (missionaries), first to ferret out secret performances of ceremonies and then to disrupt them. Lastly, to complete the "preemptive strikes," these soldiers of the christian god would destroy all religious artifacts that were seized in the process. While these missionaries had no official sanction to perform such civil police services, they were never restrained by civil authorities but, rather, appear to have been greatly appreciated in their vigilante activities.

These outlawed ceremonies quite often continued in one fashion or another in spite of attempts to end their observance. They were performed in hidden locations, often in abbreviated form, and often transformed in other ways to make concealment and continuation possible. One particular category of Lakota ceremony became a nighttime ceremony, which is, even now, typically conducted in complete darkness, a remnant of the earlier necessity for concealment. The perseverance of these ceremonial forms and of Indian cultures in general in the face of such intense repression and oppression is itself a testament to the tenacity of Indian peoples and their ongoing commitment to resistance and struggle. Needless to say, the combined efforts of church and state to rid North America of pagan Indian ceremonial life never quite succeeded.

With the intensification of the modern indigenous movement of resistance, beginning in the 1960s and reaching an apex in the emergence of the American Indian Movement after 1968,[1] a renewed pride in Indian identity began to erupt, and not coincidentally, this invigorated Indian pride was accompanied by a renewed interest in the ancient ceremonial life of the peoples. What had been hidden or practiced by only a few in remote locations for so long, suddenly began to claim a place in the public consciousness of Indian communities in one nation after another, with Lakota ceremonial practice taking center stage among both urban Indians and New Age Whites. What had been revived as a tourist attraction at Pine Ridge in the sixties was brought back into the open as a legitimate ceremony. No longer produced as mere voyeuristic spectacle, and with stricter and more traditional observance, Sun Dances in the seventies took place at Porcupine and Kyle on the Pine Ridge Reservation, and at Ironwood Hilltop and Crow Dog's Paradise on the Rosebud. With this spiritual renaissance, Indian identity was rekindled with a new pride, which became more and more intimately connected with the Indian political resistance of the day. This renaissance of Indian traditional ceremonial life has continued unabated even today and shows little sign of ebbing soon. It speaks to the persistent and enduring attachment of Indian people to their traditional cultures and structuring of society.

Yet there is also a cost to pay related to the extant, complex, and interminably lingering affects that european and euro-american colonization has on the well-being of Indian communities. The emergence of Indian ceremonial traditions into the larger public consciousness has generated a sexy appeal of the exotic among the spiritually exhausted colonizer communities of North America and Europe, resulting in yet another invasion of Indian peoples. This time the invasion is not a colonial attempt to appropriate Indian lands; rather, this invasion intrudes on the intimate and private religious space of Indian communities who are at the same time trying to heal themselves from five hundred years of colonial abuse. In this moment of late-colonial capitalism, the invaders see their intentions as benign, yet the effect is a globalization of private community acts as a new commodity fetish.[2]

This essay will look at the non-Indian appropriation of Indian ceremonial life as a means of unraveling some of the complexity.

Commitment and Vicarious Suffering

All Indian ceremonies contain some aspect of commitment—both to the ceremony itself, that is, to the spiritual presence that empowers a particular ceremony, and to the community in the context of which the ceremony is performed.[3] Many ceremonies also contain some aspect of vicarious suffering. While the purpose of the suffering is usually expressed in terms of some benefit for the community whole, its intensity can be of considerable magnitude for the individual. The strong sense of "doing" is part of what makes these ceremonies so appealing to American Indians as oppressed peoples living in these late stages of colonization and conquest.[4] In the midst of political and social hopelessness marked by extreme poverty in today's Indian communities, and continued pressures from the systemic power structure of church and state, which continues to press Indian peoples today toward a standard of compliance with the terms of colonization, these ceremonies provide hope for Indian peoples. It is in the commitment and the doing of these ceremonies that many Indian people achieve some sense of doing something concrete about their community's ongoing experience of injustice, degradation, alienation, and all the dysfunction that emerges from successive generations of colonial imposition. In the suffering we experience in these ceremonies, there is hope for the people, and our pain is short by comparison to the pain of the community. The suffering in these ceremonies (called "self-mutilation" or "self-torture" in the "professional" literature) is always an act engaged in by personal choice, and the personal commitment is always made for the sake of the people.

Vicarious suffering of any Indian person on behalf of the community is also part of the ritual drama typical of the Purification Ceremony, or Sweat Lodge as it is colloquially known. In this ceremony, the heat can be so intense for so long that the participants must encourage each other to "remember" why they are there, to concentrate on their prayers and not focus on their own pain. Some euro-americans have asked over the years whether this ceremony is similar to a sauna. While I have never *prayed* in a sauna and therefore find the question somewhat bewildering, I can attest that the Purification Ceremony is typically a couple of hours longer than the ten-minute sauna stay recommended by physicians, and it is certainly much hotter. The lodge itself is a symbolic microcosm of the earth. Our suffering is the substance of our prayer and is willingly endured for the sake of the earth and all of our relatives who live on it. Our prayer is especially for the community in which we thrive; we pray first of all for our tribal nation and then for all our relatives—black, red, yellow, and White; two-leggeds, four-leggeds, wingeds, and all the living moving things from rocks and trees to mountains and lakes.

Likewise, the Rite of Vigil (often referred to by New Agers and others as "Vision Quest") requires a commitment to a period of rigorous fasting—abstaining from both food and water—while bivouacked on a hillside far from the center of the community, confined in a small ceremonially marked area, perhaps a body length and a half in length and width. The duration of the ceremony varies from a single day and night, perhaps for an adolescent completing the first Rite of Vigil, to a more typical four-day period in the modern context. Stories are told of people in ancient times regularly completing ceremonies lasting six days and even up to ten or eleven days, far in excess of what modern medical science would allow as possible without the replenishing of body fluids.

While I have made a conscious choice *not* to provide an "instruction manual" for Indian ceremonial life and therefore do not intend to discuss the

technical aspects of the spiritual experiences associated with these ceremonies, it should be apparent enough that the spiritual commitment needed
to complete such a regimen far exceeds the physical requirements. While
there is always a personal benefit from completing this ceremony, and even
personal accretions of spiritual power, these benefits are always experienced
as intended to help that person in her or his commitment to the well-being of
the whole. In other words, the individual learns how she or he can better
serve the community and contribute to its health and perpetuation. In the
Lakota context, for instance, the community typically will greet the individual upon completion of the ceremony not with an exclamation of "congratu-
lations," but rather with a simple handshake and the words *thank you*—thank
you, because the community has benefited from the person's successful completion of the commitment.

While variations of both of these ceremonies are common to a great many
Indian nations in North America, the Sun Dance is a more regional ceremony
native to the Great Plains and Great Basin regions of the western United
States. Again, one commits to this ceremony on behalf of the community
whole, even when each participant has personal reasons for having initiated
the commitment. As with the Rite of Vigil, the Sun Dance ceremony involves
a pledge by the dancer to personal deprivation (no food and no water) and the
physical effort of sustained dancing over a three- or four-day period, depending on the particular national tradition,[5] through the heat of midsummer days
and sometimes with dancing even extending through the night. In the Lakota
tradition, the vicarious nature of the ceremony is captured in a common accla-
mation, "That the people might live!"[6] The ceremony is sometimes referred to
as an annual world renewal ceremony and can be described as a ceremony for
maintaining the balance and harmony of life. Thus, whatever the personal
reasons for a dancer's commitment to the ceremony, the good of community
and its well-being are always most prominently at stake.

Colonialism, Neocolonialism, and Resistance

These ceremonies are three of the most common ceremonies practiced today
by a variety of Indian peoples, including urban multitribal Indian communities, but by no means are they the only ceremonies that have been revived. In
this climate of persistent psychological and emotional colonization, they have
become symbolic of our continuing cultural resistance to the colonizer at religious, social, and political levels. While important aspects of spiritual power
are associated with the ceremonies, they also have a distinct political and

social power that is simultaneously derived from and reifying to the cohesion of the community and its focus on resistance and liberation.

Countless Indians on virtually every U.S. reservation have been withdrawing from the christian churches into which they had been missionized and are returning to these sorts of traditional ceremonies. The incongruity of maintaining Indian self-pride and self-conscious identity as "Indian" communities while participating in a religion imposed on us by our colonizer finally began to break down the inroads made by several generations of missionary imposition on our Indian communities.

Many younger Indian clergy and some of the congregations they serve have moved to reshape the christianity they have embraced. They are doing this by reinterpreting of the european and euro-american theological and faith categories in language and material forms that better reflect our Indian identity. Yet for the majority, this shift is inadequate and still leaves the colonized with a religious tradition that belongs to and derives from the colonizer. In the unhealthy and dysfunctional colonized world that we Indian people inhabit in North America today, it seems that the healthiest persons are those who have engaged in full-voiced resistance to the continuing colonization of Indian peoples and have found a return to traditional ceremonial life to be a significant part of this resistance. Thus, the boldest of the younger Indian clergy have hearkened to the call of these traditionalists and can be found participating in the traditional ceremonies, praying in ways that an earlier generation of missionaries would have criticized as devil worship.

Indian Religious Traditions as Commodity
in a Mass Consumption Society

The young man had wandered in early to the site of an urban Indian community religious ceremony. The ceremonial leader met the man cordially. Because of the colonial phenomenon of "mixed blood," it is often impossible to ascertain by sight whether a person is Indian, so the leader asked the man whether he was Indian and what tribe he might be. The young man's honest reply was, "No, I am just a White man who is a *pipe carrier*." Just as easily and genuinely, the leader responded by asking, "Oh, yes? For whom do you carry that pipe? For what community?" In possession of an Indian community religious symbol, but living a polar opposite existence in the non-Indian world, this young White man had no answer to the question but, rather, had to ask the meaning of the question. In reality, he knew for whom he carried this pipe; he carried it for himself and for his own spiritual empowerment. Someone had sold this young man a pipe and a bill of goods to go with it.

Colonization and the processes of forcing assimilation are not yet finished with Indian peoples. Even as we seek new ways to embrace ourselves as Indian communities, the colonizer has found new ways to impede Indian healing and to steal away what is left of Indian identity, cultural values, and traditional life-ways. The gravity of these latest and most deceptive attempts to neutralize and assimilate Indians into euro-american normative culture cannot be overstated: they are nothing less than "spiritual racism" and "theological vandalism."[7] This newest threat to Indian well-being actually builds on the impoverishment that has been established by five centuries of invasion and conquest, yet it involves a seeming affirmation of Indian cultures. Perversely, however, it includes its inculcation with a robust strain of the mass consumption virus. The appeal of easy cash accumulation for individuals who are accustomed to poverty is sometimes too great to refuse.

Over the past three decades, euro-american entrepreneurs have discovered that Indian culture has a dramatic appeal to those New Age aficionados whose sense of spiritual poverty has whetted their appetites for the exotic and reduced their economic wealth proportionately. First Carlos Castaneda and then Lynn Andrews found that even wholly fabricated but exotically romanticized tales of Indian mysteries could gain them both academic credibility and wealth at the same time.[8] These parodies of Indian spiritual traditions have spawned countless imitations, some of whom have gained credibility by spending a short time in actual Indian ceremonies, indulging their fantasies. As I mentioned in chapter 3, there has come a report from the Florida American Indian Movement that a White woman using the catchy Indian-sounding name of Bear, after having danced in a Lakota Sun Dance ceremony, had established herself in the how-to workshop business, drawing 250 people at $1,500 per person. The susceptible are quickly separated from their wallets in return for some illusion of spiritual well-being, Indian people are left the poorer as misperceptions and falsified interpretations of our world are sold for profit. Thus, as we noted, Indian cultural traditions, particularly those identified as spiritual or religious traditions, have emerged as commodities of trade in the Great American Supermarket of Spirituality.

With this discovery of Indian spirituality as a growth industry, many Indian people with a little knowledge—that is, significantly more authentic knowledge than Castaneda or Andrews possess—began to move into the marketplace as well. While Andrews and Castaneda made up fantasies that sounded Indian but were actually fabricated lies, the Indian purveyors of spirituality are also engaged in selling a lie. In their case, the lie is decorated with enough genuine Indian forms and structures that the purchasers are led to believe that they are indeed buying the genuine item. Yet there remains a significant and substantial set of differences between euro-american New Age belief structures and those of Indian peoples. For the purposes of this essay, I would like to describe a single but definitive distinction between the two.

New Age Individualism and Indian Community: A Colonial Clash of Values

Beginning already with Aristotle (in the fourth century B.C.E.), but accelerated by the next generation of hellenistic philosophers (Stoics, Epicureans, Skeptics) from 300 B.C.E. on, mediterranean thinking and, hence, european thinking took a decided turn toward the emergence of the individual. With the conquest of Alexander the Great, Aristotle's pupil, Europe began to experience the steady decline of the importance of community. The city-state was supplanted by empire followed by empire, and greek philosophy shifted subtly away from Aristotle's search for the "good" toward the hellenistic search for the wise individual. Both religion (the "mystery religions") and philosophy in the three centuries leading up to the emergence of christianity became increasingly concerned with the salvation of or the behavior of the individual, a trajectory that led directly to the emergence of the cartesian "self" more than a millennium and a half later (and the ludic postmodern American selfish self at the end of the second millennium C.E.).[9]

It should be of little surprise then to discover in New Age aficionados a spiritual focus on the self and the engagement of spiritual experience for the sake of personal (that is, individual) self-enhancement or the accrual of personal spiritual power. Whether this is good or ill is beyond the purview of this essay. I only intend to emphasize that this modus operandi is diametrically opposed to ceremonial intentionality in any American Indian traditional cultural context.

When New Age aficionados invade Indian ceremonies, they represent another sort of colonizing virus that threatens the health and well-being of the communities into which they have invited themselves or from whom they have finagled an invitation from Indian people unaccustomed to saying no and too weak from generations of colonization to change their traditional cultural habit of hospitality, even when their own cultural and physical survival might depend on it. Many of these spiritual seekers are genuinely well intentioned and seriously searching for something more substantial than the spiritual experiences of the church into which they were born and raised, or they seek

a more life-affirming and meaningful experience than is available in their secular society. Typically, they see themselves as sharing a worldview with Indian
people, including concern for environmental issues, openness to the universe
as some expression of pervasive divinity, a sense of the interrelationship of all
things, especially all people, and a sense of the immanence and accessibility of
spiritual power. All these may be thought of as laudable, yet however laudable
these beliefs, they are still White, euro-american thoughts rather than Indian
thoughts. They cannot transform these persons into Indians, and indeed the
New Age seeker may find her- or himself as embodying the distinct opposite of
what Indian religious traditions represent. Namely, the New Ager is a prime
example of the western, european, euro-american cultural value of individualism in its starkest naïveté.[10]

The viral aspect of this introduction is that the individualist belief that the
New Age adherent carries into and imposes on an Indian community can very
quickly affect that indigenous community—and is frighteningly reminiscent
of the disease-infested blankets and the like that were brought into villages
and communities in the past. Especially vulnerable to the doctrine of individualism, with its promises of "freedom" and wealth, is the younger generation
of that indigenous community. This is a common experience in all Indian communities, but especially in urban centers, because Indian people there may
not have readily available access to traditional teaching elders. Thus, we have
a generation of young people who are learning, or mis-learning, how to be
Indian from non-Indian individualists. New Agers, to this extent, are finally
much more effective in destroying Indian cultural values than several generations of missionaries and government functionaries have been, especially in
this late period of (neo-) colonialism.

Christianizing the Language of Ceremonial Traditions

As the euro-american virus of individualism infects Indian traditional communities, the final conquest of the colonizer is most apparent in the changes
that occur in the ways that Indian people themselves talk about their ceremonies. This shift to individualism, marked by a person's participation in a
ceremony with the intention of gaining personal power, is what I refer to as
the christianizing of Indian religious traditions. It represents the newest and
most insidious colonization of the American Indian mind, one that may or may
not be immediately recognizable by the person whose mind is so affected. The
gospel of this christianizing process is not Jesus but the euro-american/chris-
tian cultural value of individualism with its embedded capitalist propensities.

The result of this christianizing process is to further erode the Indian value of community and to bring us one step closer to the modern globalization of culture that is grounded in and molded by euro-western values. The surface structures of our ceremonies may continue to look Indian, but the deep structure of meaning that undergirds the ceremony is slowly changing and eroding traditional values and patterns of behavior.

Most critically, the infestation of individualism that comes with the New Age invasion of Indian ceremonies means that there is a subtle degeneration in our language, which serves to spread the virus. Language degeneration even spreads among the teaching elders and spiritual leaders of a community as they struggle to translate their culture and the meaning of their ceremonies into language that can be accessed (and often accessed for money) by those euro-White intruders who come to our ceremonies out of such a radically different set of cultural behaviors and values.

As I have already noted, it is very difficult for Indian people to say no. This is especially true when the White supplicant comes into an Indian ceremonial context with greater economic resources than either the spiritual leader or the local Indian people in general. Even without engaging in the active marketing and selling of ceremonies, the spiritual leader may find him- or herself the recipient of some financial benefit. However small that benefit may be, it has a great impact in an environment of poverty, and this impact is felt not only by the particular recipient; the entire community is thrown into greater disharmony than already exists. Yet with the appearance of the first of these euro-american supplicants, the degradation of language about the ceremony already begins, as the spiritual elder changes the language of explanation in order to accommodate an outsider with money.

I am not arguing that these traditional spiritual leaders intend to change the meaning of the ceremony. The fact is that the ceremonies do change over time, but this occurs as a natural process inherent in their organic composition and purpose, and as a result of the adaptations made by the spiritual teachers of the communities in accordance with the changing times and situations brought on by virtue of the Fourth World existence of American Indian peoples. Indeed, Smith recalls a soliloquy by Betonie in Leslie Marmon Silko's *Ceremony*, in which Betonie reminds us that something that doesn't "change and grow" is dead.[11] Rather, as this deceptively debilitating adjustment is manifested, their language about ceremony changes gradually as each elder struggles to communicate with the insistent outsider, struggles to translate precepts and concepts of one culture to make them comprehensible to another. It seems to be a natural colonizing process that the colonized shift their language in order to accommodate the understanding of the colonizer. Yet I should clarify here that this "natural" process is really an unnatural process of oppression and conquest that has inherently logical and devastating effects on both the colonized and colonizer. It reifies the false inferior status of the colonized while simultaneously reifying the equally illegitimate status of superiority of the colonizer. So it becomes a natural response on the part of the oppressed to accommodate power! As a result, the traditional elder may make small shifts in her or his language, shifts so small that they may be imperceptible even to the elder. Yet slowly, the meaning of the ceremony is christianized toward the western, christian valorization and privileging of the individual. Eventually, the young from the elder's own community pick up this new language, unaware that it is new or that it represents a concession to the dearth of understanding on the part of colonizer participants; the virus of individualism has suddenly gained a firmer foothold. And just as suddenly, it seems, the ceremony is engaged by members of the community in order to enhance the personal spiritual well-being or power of the individual, rather than the well-being of the community.

The net result is a tragic loss for both Indian peoples and for euro-americans. For the former, a way of life is changed forever; for the latter, they have paid out bundles of dollars in return for the purchase of an illusion of Indianness, for a spiritual experience that they can display with pride but that has little actual meaning or validity in terms of what is actually claimed. For American Indian communities, the result is a loss of culture and the erosion of the system of values inherent in the historic indigenous traditions that have given the people strength to resist the full power of colonization until now. For euro-americans and europeans, the addiction to power and dominance is enhanced as they take the illusive surface structure of Indian ceremonies and colonize them into just another religious resource for themselves, a resource clothed with the appearance of righteousness, much as statutory rape can be clothed with the claim of prior mutual consent.

What we are experiencing in the Indian world is the globalization of ourselves as a commodity and the concomitant transformation of our cultures toward an emerging world culture defined by market symbols of global consumption similar to the McDonald's, Nike, Pizza Hut, and Sony billboards in every major Third World city. Perhaps technology will eventually provide for a new spirituality that will satisfy the contemporary Star Trek mentality. Unfortunately, there may be no alternative as the globalized, christianized indigenous religions of the world lose their antiquity, efficacy, and the cultural value base upon which they have always been predicated.

American Indian Generosity
and Spiritual Scalp Collecting

At a deeply philosophical level, then, the question must be raised: Can and should non-Indians—particularly the colonizer/settler class of euro-western Whites—participate in the ceremonial spirituality of American Indian peoples? This question seems ever-present these days in my classroom, in discussion at lectures, and in mail that comes daily across my desk. For the most part, the question is articulated by people whose sincerity I do not question. They voice, at least, a great respect for the ceremonies, but they also express a deep-felt need for their individual participation in Pipe Ceremonies, "Sweat Lodge" purification rites, Sun Dances, and a variety of other events. Many of these nonnatives have come to see American Indian ceremonial spirituality as somehow essential to their own well-being.

For their part, Indians have responded in a variety of ways across a broad spectrum of possibilities. Many, especially a number of Lakota practitioners, have welcomed non-Indian participation and have come increasingly to consider their spirituality as a human universal. Finding their knowledge eminently marketable, these spiritual salespersons have become virtual missionaries or counter-missionaries as they develop converts and followers in places as far removed from their own lands as Oregon and Germany.[12] They have made the teaching of native spirituality a for-profit industry servicing a spiritually starved if materially saturated euro-american clientele. While they inevitably alienate themselves from their own people, there are financial rewards that become especially lucrative if they take their show to Malibu, Marin County, Boulder, Aspen, or Germany. There continue to be significant communities of Indian people, however, who resist both these spirituality evangelists and the economic impetuses, and who continue to see their ceremonial life as community events closed to outsiders.[13]

Since opinion seems so divided among American Indian practitioners themselves, a corollary question becomes even more important: Who are the appropriate spokespersons for giving an authoritative answer to the first question? Nonnatives who have participated in native ceremonies invariably announce that they were, in fact, invited by Indian people themselves to participate. The invitation, in a sense, becomes their passport into the spiritual world of Indian peoples. The actuality is that hospitality is one of the most important virtues in every Indian community. This makes it most difficult for Indian people to say no, even when it means the invasion of ceremonial privacy and sometimes even when we do want to say no. Non-Indians seem, correspondingly, to have difficulty in not taking advantage of Indian peoples in any context, even taking advantage of extreme generosity. It can be argued that euro-american people are culturally good at taking what they want or think they need but have great difficulty in receiving any gift, especially if understanding the boundaries of the gift is implicit in the giving, and further, that euro-americans are best at imposing on others rather than offering their own gifts. Somehow, it is never quite clear to the colonizer that there are some things that we do not want to share.

Even in those cases, however, where a non-Indian has a clear invitation from an Indian participant, the question must be raised whether the Indian person has the right to extend the invitation. In any euro-american context, of course, the invitation of one individual to another individual can be taken at face value as a valid and authentic invitation, which the other person may accept or not merely on the basis of personal preference. The complicating factor in the American Indian ceremonial context is the community. Since the ceremony is a community event and all participants affect the entire community and its ceremony, who does have the right to invite a nonmember into the intimacy and privacy of the community's ceremony? While this complexity should be a warning to all of us in the Indian community in terms of our sense of generosity, it should also be taken seriously by our euro-american relatives. Any non-Indian who is so invited needs to question seriously within her- or himself whether the invitation is even remotely valid and genuine—even if it comes from an elder or leader who seems to hold high status. And perhaps, before even expressing interest in experiencing someone else's intimate spiritual relationships, individuals should also engage a personal examination of their own motives for wanting to do such a thing.

Generosity: A Dysfunctional Virtue

I have already begun to suggest that the enduring results of colonialism have left Indian people fighting with chronic levels of dysfunction that may lead to inappropriate invitations to intimacy, as do many other abuse survivors in our modern world of violence. Indeed, we find quite often that the very values our cultures have always lived can actually exacerbate our dysfunction when they are lived too uncritically in our modern relationship with our colonizer. This is to say, even virtues can ultimately prove to have a dysfunctional potential, especially in our contemporary world of colonial power and transition. The Indian valorizing of the virtue of generosity, as we have already begun to see, is one example.

The missionaries who intended to civilize American Indian peoples found much to criticize in Indian cultures. The propensity of families in many Indian cultures to periodically give away all or much of their accumulated wealth consistently came under missionary attack as diabolical. Since the church has always intended that people's generosity extend primarily to itself (i.e., the church), one can sense how a people's generosity toward one another may have presented a significant threat to the church. The missionaries, as well as other european and euro-american observers, were further appalled to witness a giveaway for which the giver(s) demanded nothing in return. This was an abomination in light of the precepts of individualism, capitalism, and civilization. Be that as it may, generosity is counted as one of the cardinal virtues by nearly all Indian peoples.

In my own tribe, traditional leadership on the council of "little old ones," the *no^nho^n'zhi^nga*, was contingent upon proving oneself with regard to this virtue of generosity. For instance, a candidate for appointment to the council will have given away all that his (and occasionally her) family has on at least three occasions.[14] Along with bravery, intelligence, and community morality, generosity helped to define those who were paradigmatic for the whole community. Another excellent and historical example occurred in the Northeast of what is now the United States. The open generosity of Indian peoples in New England upon the first arrival of english colonizers is both well known and well documented. Without the agricultural skill and generosity of the original inhabitants of the land, the colonists would have certainly perished during their first winters in North America.[15] To this day, to admire something in another's possession quite often results in receiving it as a gift. Such an ethic proved to be foreign and alienating to the missionaries, even as it proved useful in building solid community existence and alliances within and among Indian nations.

While the virtue of generosity, as it is practiced by different American Indian peoples, can be touted as something superior to the values of civilization that have been imposed on Indian peoples by the europeans, it has also become susceptible to abuse in two significant ways: it has been misappropriated by our White relatives and misdirected by Indian peoples themselves. The inability of Indian people to say no, for instance, to the White, New Age invasion of Indian spirituality leaves our communities extremely vulnerable. The ethic of generosity dictates that we share what we have with all those who come our way. Food is always shared with a guest who happens to drop by, so it is only natural that the gift we treasure most highly, meaning our spirituality, can also be so easily and generously offered to others. What we are dealing with today is a *spiritual* giveaway in which Indian generosity has been pressed to an extreme of dysfunction. Moreover, as we seem to invite more and more of our White relatives to join us in our traditional ceremonial life, the very ceremonies that give us life are being degraded before our eyes, even though we do not usually recognize the change.

In the modern context of unrelenting euro-american conquest and colonization, American Indians have suffered significantly high levels of social disturbance and mental health dysfunction, from chronic, communitywide levels of depression to widespread alcoholism, high rates of teen suicides,[16] serious alienation from the euro-american culture of work and achievement,[17] and an ongoing colonization of our minds. One result of this process is a pervasive codependency with our colonizer,[18] resulting in what I would characterize as a serious addiction to the color White. There is a constant need for approval of White institutions (especially government and church), White authority figures, and White friends. Thus, when euro-american clamor for acceptance into our ceremonies, all too often we are flattered and feel a sense of affirmation for our culture and our religious traditions instead of being wary, guarded, suspicious, and distrusting.

The codependent need for approval on the part of the abused person is a common theme in contemporary mental health analysis. In the same way, Indian people, struggling with our own history of the paternalistic abuse of colonialism, seem to have some underlying need for White approval. Indian churches clamor for the approval of White bishops; Indian national government figures clamor for the approval of Washington, D.C., and its array of senators and congresspersons; Indian national community agency employees all clamor to meet the approval of the U.S. government's BIA or Indian Health Service bureaucracies. And always, we are susceptible to the well-meaning, liberal do-gooders who want so much to help us and tell us what is best for Indian peoples. White greed compounds this Indian dysfunction in the rape of our natural resources, particularly in extraction contracts that are entirely too favorable to the multinational conglomerates that enrich themselves almost at will on many reservations.[19] Likewise, the New Age aficionados move into our world, exuding flattering words of affirmation about the spiritual treasures of Indian peoples, and then proceed to steal those treasures just as they stole the land a generation or two earlier.

Many kindhearted Indian persons respond in this codependent relationship out of a felt need to help our White relatives find their way spiritually. Yet it seems that there is an even stronger felt need to garner the approval and affirmation of these same spiritually impoverished White friends.

Concluding Concerns

Only with some understanding of the complexity of late-colonial relationships and the exotic appeal of Indian ceremonies in our contemporary world can we begin to raise and address some of the most critical concerns. To that end, I will conclude this essay with a list of five concerns that I believe to be most pertinent. They are drawn from the context of a simple question: Is the sharing of Indian ceremonial life ultimately helpful to either Indian or non-Indian people?

1. Cross-cultural differences make it very difficult for non-Indians to internalize Indian meanings relating to ceremonial acts. This makes it necessary for Indian structures to be remodeled accordingly around non-Indian cultural structures and ideas in order to include non-Indian "individuals."

2. As a result, the euro-american participant can only assume a superficial participation in the ceremony, that is, at the level of surface structure. There is profound deep-structure significance, of course, for both Indian and non-Indian participants in a ceremony, but the deep-structure significance is necessarily quite different for each. The sense of individual spiritual self-enhancement that is so central to euro-american participants, i.e., New Agers, means that they experience only the illusion of Indianness and the illusion of spiritual power. The result is not at all real, or to the extent that the experience is real, it is no longer in any way Indian because it has been radically individualized.

3. Along with the communalist/individualist cultural difference comes another significant difference that is regularly overlooked by New Age wannabes. Namely, American Indian national communities are what anthropologists often refer to as modal social organizations, as opposed to sodal social organizations. This means that Indian nationality, and hence participation in the ceremonial spirituality of the community, is not a voluntary act such as joining a church. Rather, the concept of modality signifies that membership in the community is a birthright. This means that euro-americans who invite themselves into Indian ceremonies enjoy a privilege that we Indian people do not and cannot enjoy. Euro-americans are able to choose their tribe of presumed affiliation from among a wide range of choices, whereas Indian people are stuck, so to speak, with the tribe of their birth. For the New Ager, choosing Indian spirituality and choosing a particular Indian community whose spirituality they will imitate is much like choosing a church denomination or congregation. That, of course, is the history of voluntary organization in the United States, dating especially from the eighteenth century. Indian people choose neither tribe nor clan. We are what we are by birth.

4. In many cultures, spiritual knowledge is not the universal right of all citizens in the national community, but there is a division of labor according to clans and societies. In many cultures, different clans or societies have particular responsibilities for parts of a national ceremony and, thus, possess partic-

ular knowledge not necessarily shared by all in the community. The success of the ceremony in this case depends on the appropriate participation of each clan and society in the nation, as each performs its discrete role in the ceremonial whole. Not only does the whole community depend on each subgroup to do its part, but the knowledge associated with each part also belongs to the particular clan or society that is responsible for performing it. Other clans, other family members, and other neighbors may indeed have no right to even "know" any part of that knowledge. The Hopi spokesperson Talayesva, for instance, declines to comment on such knowledge when pressed by Simmons, the anthropologist, on exactly such a basis.[20] The sentiment expressed either explicitly or implicitly as "I have a right to know!" is an inherently White and euro-american valorization of the individual, whether that individual is an anthropologist or some other sort of scientific scholar, New Age aficionado, or even an ostensibly curious "student." "I have a right to know" is countered by the communitarian interest in the good of the whole. Demanding the individual's presumed right to know can violate the good of the whole, especially when that right to know is being pressed by someone from outside of the community itself.

5. Essentially, I have argued that White participation in Indian community ceremonial actions contributes to the ongoing destruction of Indian culture, ceremonies, and communities and constitutes continued colonization in a time that is often referred to as postcolonial.

Finally, White participation in Indian ceremonial life reinforces the socially constructed notions of White privilege so prevalent and dominant in our larger societal whole. White involvement in Indian ceremonies is actually harmful to our White relatives because it reinforces the inbred sense of White privilege that is the birth heritage of every White person in North America, just as male privilege is the inescapable birth heritage of every male. The intensity of the social construction is such that even as liberals attempt to disavow their own privileging, they cannot escape it. One can hear the appeal to White privilege in the seemingly neutral claim of many of our White relatives: "Spirituality does not belong to anyone." Yet the neutrality dissolves as one understands the claim as a White claim on Indian spirituality and either the replication of our ceremonies or direct participation in them. "You must share," is a second claim, one that holds us to a dysfunctional valorization of our own cultural value of hospitality. Yet it needs to be emphasized that we hurt our White relatives and friends when we naively invite them into our private, community ceremonial life. We are only encouraging the final act of colonization and conquest. In an amazing but convenient turnaround, our ceremonies are no longer castigated as demonic, savage, and uncivilized; instead, with Indian land and natural resources already plundered, our ceremonies have become the new prize possession of the colonizer, and their theft the ultimate act of postmodern colonialism.[21] It is a new version of the colonizer indulgence in colonial exoticism, in other words, a fetishization of Indian people and Indian traditions.[22] This becomes a primary reason for arguing that the inclusion of White folk in the community intimacy of our ceremonies is not healthy for those White relatives, especially if they really do want to make a difference in the world and find creative ways to do things differently.

5

Fools and Fools Crow

The Colonialism of Thomas Mails's
Fools Crow: Wisdom and Power

That colonialism and its particular types of racism continue in academia and in popular american religion seems to be little recognized, at least outside of American Indian communities. This short chapter and the next take a look at this phenomenon through the critical review of two books.[1] The first, *Fools Crow: Wisdom and Power* by Thomas Mails, is a popular book about a recently deceased Lakota medicine man of considerable repute. The second, Stephen E. Feraca's *Wakinyan: Lakota Religion in the Twentieth Century*, presents itself as more academic in nature, as an anthropological study of Lakota religion. Both texts promise much more than they finally are able to deliver; yet most readers will not have the necessary tools or understanding to sort out truth from fictions that sound authoritative and make such bold claims to truth.[2]

Frank Fools Crow was a celebrated and long-lived Oglala leader, who died in 1989, a few months short of a hundred years of age. He was a traditional chief and a spiritual leader among his people for nearly three-quarters of a century, and his funeral was attended by celebrities from the White world and by White religious leaders from roman catholic and protestant churches. The volume discussed here is the second book about Fools Crow written by Thomas Mails, an author who published considerable New Age–style writings about American Indians.

One might have hoped that fifteen years' added maturity would have generated a book that reflected less of the White, star-struck romanticism that colored Mails's first volume about Frank Fools Crow. Such was not to be the case. Ward Churchill captures the general sentiment exquisitely in his critique of Jerry Mander's *In the Absence of the Sacred: The Failure of Technology and the Survival of the Indian Nations* (1991): "They just can't help it. I swear, they really can't. It's too deeply ingrained in the subconscious, a matter of truly subliminal presumption."[3] Mails's newest book will be appealing and even irresistible to New Age aficionados and Lakota wannabes. The late author has been one of the leading White profiteers of commodified American-Indian-ish New Age spirituality, and the opening line of the book announces immediately that we are dealing here with (euro-) individualized self-aggrandizement above all else: "What you are about to read may be the rarest document ever published about a Native American holy man" (9).

This book belongs to a particular genre of modern gnostic fantasy, much like the works of Lynn Andrews or Carlos Castaneda.[4] While Mails's subject—unlike those of Andrews's first book, *Medicine Woman*, or Castenada's Don Juan in *The Teachings of Don Juan*—was an actual human being, Mails's subject has conveniently died, making validation of his writing impossible. Supposedly, Fools Crow had "given" Mails two different kinds of information. The first was information that was to be made public immediately and constituted his initial *Fools Crow* volume (published in the late 1970s).[5] The second kind, more esoteric (and fantastic, as it turns out), however, was to be withheld until after his death. Hence, *Fools Crow: Wisdom and Power*.

After an opening apologetic that argues Mails's lofty stature as the only authentic heir to Fools Crow's wisdom and medicine, the book unfolds as an explicit instruction manual on Fools Crow's spiritual power. For those whose exotic fantasy is to experiment with Indian medicine, the manual will have certain appeal. More significant, however, is the privileged place Mails carves out for himself with repeated self-serving references throughout the narrative to his particular place of privilege—or rather presumed place of privilege—with Mr. Fools Crow. Early in the book, Mails entertains the thought that "some will wonder why Fools Crow chose to entrust me with this extraordinary information" (11). The arrogance of Mails's White paternalism becomes apparent in his insistence that, first, only he is privy to this secret knowledge, and second, he is the only remaining living authority figure for Fools Crow's wisdom (27 *et inter alia*) and for the authentic Sun Dance tradition of the Lakota (22, 27). Thus, he goes so far as to place himself, in intellectual and spiritual acumen, above all living Lakota medicine people and spiritual elders ("He did not invite other medicine men to sit with us.")[6] and finally includes himself as Fools Crow's equal!

> Perhaps I can best explain the relationship that Fools Crow and I
> had by the fact that he asked me to call him by his first name,

Frank, and not "grandfather," or "grandpa," as everyone else did. He knew that I had not come to sit at his feet to be his student or patient, and that he was never, in any sense, my mentor. . . . Somehow, and the methods used are revealed herein, *Wakan-Tanka* told Fools Crow that I was that one who could and would do this. (11–12)

Whatever his relationship with Mr. Fools Crow and whatever name he used to address him in person, to use his first name in a formal publication is utterly disrespectful—to Mr. Fools Crow and to Indian people generally, given the great deference in which people in his own community held him and still hold him. On the other hand, it would seem that Mails simply failed to understand Fools Crow's great sense of humor, so deeply rooted in use of the ironic. Perhaps the exchange went something like this: "What should I call you?" "Call me Frank. You are not my grandson. And, as a white man, you haven't earned the right of relationship to call me grandfather." Of course, the more contemporary phenomenon is for many Indian elders to take egotistic pride in having New Age Whites trek to their doorsteps and call them by the relationship term of *Grandpa* or *Grandma*. And given the great disturbance of Indian stability caused by 512 years of invasion, colonization, land theft, and the like, why should these elders not take some liberties with White admirers?

In Mails's opinion, Fools Crow was the "greatest Native American holy person to live during the last one hundred years" (9), greater than even Black Elk—a.k.a. Mr. Nicholas Black Elk, the Oglala catholic catechist who was given the baptismal name of Nicholas and who was also an uncle of Mr. Fools Crow.[7] Greatest, in this case, seems to have more to do with having been published, since Black Elk was not considered at all to have been the greatest even of his peers. Indeed, "greatest" does not seem to be as important a category of cognition for Lakota peoples or other Native Americans as it is for Mails and his White american culture. Indeed, different medicine people have different gifts and work with different spirits and hence have different sorts of power to accomplish different kinds of healing and helping. A healthy and holistic Indian community needs a full variety of these special people in order to survive. Fools Crow was indeed a special gift to his people, but he was one of a long line of wise and powerful interpreters or medicine men among the Oglala.

The book must be critiqued at a number of other levels, however. Technically, it would seem that, even if Mails did spend the time he claims to have spent with Fools Crow, the project should never have been attempted. It cannot help but be fraud, even with the best of intentions. Because of the cross-cultural difficulties, it was doomed from the start, simply because it relies so heavily on an oversimplification of cross-cultural translation and reconstruction. Mails himself reports a conversation with Fools Crow about John Neihardt's *Black Elk Speaks*. As Mails read from the book to Fools Crow, the latter responded, "Who is this man you are reading about? . . . That is not my uncle" (15). Mails should have learned something from the encounter. Mails's volume is not Fools Crow. Many have suggested that *Black Elk Speaks* should have better been titled *Neihardt Speaks*. So *Fools Crow: Wisdom and Power* might have more honestly been titled *Thomas Mails: Wisdom and Power*—and then left to the reader to decide whether Mails's wisdom and power were authentic or not.

Beyond the believability of Mails's claims about his relationship with Fools Crow are two related technical reasons for the book's failure: One is language and translation; the other is the matter of cross-cultural category imposition. Mails commits the mistake implicitly made by too many professional historians of religion and anthropologists. Specifically, language functions in his text as if it were culturally inconsequential for determining meaning, and that what can be said in one language must have its simple and readily accessible but codified equivalent in the interpreter's language.[8] Thus, languages become mere codes for one another. Mails's narrative of the dialogue between himself and Fools Crow belies the difficulty inherent in translating even when one is equally proficient in both languages. Mails, however, blithely proceeds: "What Fools Crow needed above all for this second kind of information was someone to help him draw out and shape what he had learned and experienced" (13), preferably, it seems, someone who spoke and understood no Lakota!

Given that Mails is not proficient in Lakota and that Fools Crow spoke only a minimal english (72)—especially with Mails—the dialogue Mails reports between them is entirely too sophisticated, not to say entirely too euro-western. Even with the presence of a translator, I would argue, the linguistic problems are insurmountable. Indeed, it becomes clear in reading the narrative that the dialogue is almost entirely an artistic creation of the author. Mails himself gives the reader a clue when he speaks of "assembling" (37) Fools Crow's thoughts, and he actually admits, "So then, this book—even when quotation marks are used—is seldom precisely what Fools Crow said, but rather what I helped him say" (14).

Ultimately, the falsification of language becomes apparent in the problem of cross-cultural category imposition. The title of chapter 1, for instance, introduces a category that Mails uses throughout the book to refer to Mr. Fools Crow: "The Old Lord of the Holy Men." This categorization of Fools Crow as "lord" imposes medieval european or earlier Mesopotamian notions of hierarchy on an American Indian figure. Used in the whole phrase *Old Lord of the Holy Men* (always capitalized), it conjures euro-western fantasies such as those authored by J. R. R. Tolkien, thus reducing Fools Crow to some european Merlinesque figure.

In another example, Mails specifically ascribes to Fools Crow the awkward english descriptor *The Highest and Most Holy One* for the Lakota *wakan tanka* (for example, 49). This usage most closely images judeo-christian references to their God and is unknown to any North American Indian community's language of the sacred. As far as I know, neither "Highest" nor "Most Holy" are ever used to define any Native American people's notion of "deity." Even the word *deity* is controversial in a Native American context. Other examples of category imposition abound and consistently put the authenticity of the book into greater and greater question. Briefly, these examples include distinguishing between "secular" and "sacred" (50), the introduction of the english/christian theological category of "faith" (43, 139), and borrowing "Higher Powers," from the euro-american theology of Alcoholics Anonymous (34 and other references).

Perhaps the most blatant example of category imposition is Mails's shameless trinitarianizing of Lakota beliefs. This was implicit throughout *Fools Crow*, the earlier book; in *Fools Crow: Wisdom and Power*, Mails eschews any pretense: "This concept of a triune God is more common to the Indians than is ordinarily believed" (35). Thus, in one fell swoop, Mails has obviated a fundamental cultural difference between his world and the indigenous world of Native America. Alfonso Ortiz may argue that American Indian peoples are "relentlessly tetradic," that is, that Indian peoples live cultures fundamentally rooted in tetradic structures—linguistically, ceremonially, politically, socially, etc. And Georges Dumezil has equally demonstrated the triadic nature of Indo-european cultures and languages. Nevertheless, Mails has miraculously discovered a human universal in his own christian doctrine of the trinity. If this is ultimately incredible to the reader, then one is pressed to think that either Mails has falsified Fools Crow or that Fools Crow was, after all, a rather thoroughgoing assimilationist and, hence, a christian (catholic) heretic rather than a traditional Lakota spiritual leader.

That we are dealing with euro-western individualism in its New Age manifestation rather than any genuine Native American or Lakota spirituality becomes succinctly clear in the final paragraph of the book:

> By keeping my promise to Frank and passing on to you this second kind of material, I place in your hands a sacred trust. As I do so, I repeat what he said—"Anyone who is willing to live the life I have led can do the

things that I do." The opportunity to meet this challenge is entirely yours. You can soar as high as you would like to in spiritual service. Who knows, *Wakan-Tanka* may even now be calling you to holiness, and to be a little hollow bone [i.e., a (Lakota) medicine man].

In the final analysis, this book belongs to the ever-growing genre of DIY (do-it-yourself), individualist spirituality that fills the shelves of the Great American supermarket of spirituality. It is marked by the arrogant confidence that even as Lakota traditional life has passed from this world with the death of Fools Crow, any White conquistador can now take over his work and become a "Lakota" *wicasa wakan*. Having killed the last of the aboriginal peoples, the killers (that is, their spiritually lost descendants) can now celebrate the theft of the aboriginals' spirituality. Thus, the book is prima facie evidence for ongoing contemporary colonialism.

6

Thunderbeings and Anthropologists
A Lakota Primer

Racialized colonialism survives in academic texts just as clearly as it surfaces in New Age commodification. As Vine Deloria Jr., Ward Churchill, Elizabeth Cook-Lynn, and others have demonstrated persistently, academics have made Indian people a means for carving out careers based on the intellectual domination of aboriginal peoples in North America, posturing themselves as the experts about the cultures of the colonized victims.[1] Their craft is, as Ojibwe scholar Gerald Vizenor insists, a trope to power, that is, power over the colonized other. The book discussed in this chapter is one current example of the continuing hegemony of White academics over their anthropological subjects.

When research fails and evidence is lacking, a convincing, made-up explanation should readily satisfy the needs of critical inquiry—when it comes to Indian peoples, at least. Stephen E. Feraca has very little to say about the *wakinyan* (thunderbeings?) in a recent book, but what he does say is written with a misguided creativity and a wholly undeserved certainty. The Lakotas, for example, have said nothing (to Feraca or to anyone else, past or present) to indicate that the bunch of cherry boughs in the crotch of the Sun Dance tree ought to be understood as the *wakinyan*'s nest. This notion Feraca has borrowed from the Cheyennes, who do make the connection. This is sufficient to convince Feraca that it must be so for Lakotas as well, and convinces him so thoroughly that he takes the word as the title of his book: *Wakinyan: Lakota Religion in the Twentieth Century.*[2]

Feraca's book is a slight revision of a very slim pamphlet of a book first published in 1963. Indeed, there is so little change in this revised edition that the reader expects that the University of Nebraska Press must necessarily regard the initial volume very highly for them to have reissued it, in a classy hardback volume, no less. The 1963 volume had been the result of a couple of summers of field research as a Columbia University master's student in the 1950s and two years' residency on the Pine Ridge Reservation as a U.S. government employee in the early 1960s. The revised edition proposes to offer the reader some updating of information that comes from another summer of research some thirty-three years later in 1996 and some minor (copy) editing, although the structure and general argument of the book, and most of the text, is essentially the same as the older version with the addition of a few explanatory footnotes. Indeed, very little new information is added to what was already only a sketchy outline, at best, of Lakota religious traditions, nor are there more than a couple of corrections of the several unmistakable errors in the original volume. In fact, some clear errors have been reemphasized as truth.

For students of Lakota traditions, there will undoubtedly be much of interest here, although very little actual new information. For Lakotas and other American Indian readers, there will continue to be much here to disappoint. Whatever one's final opinion of the book's success, it is clear that the volume has been written for that class of professional (etic) signifiers in universities and not at all for a native (emic) readership.

Wakinyan follows the Indianist genre faithfully, beginning with the obligatory chapter on the origins and modern history of the subject (object) peoples, and then discusses six particular aspects of Lakota religious traditions in the chapters that follow. This first chapter adds nothing new to the academic discourse about Lakota history except for the grudging acknowledgment that Lakotas reject the nineteenth-century "migrations" theories posited so easily as established twentieth-century fact. Thus, Feraca merely assumes, as most Lakotaists in the academy do, the veracity of those migration theories that place Lakota peoples in Minnesota until their Ojibwe enemies forced them to flee sometime in the seventeenth century.[3] Feraca fails to acknowledge the growing research and body of literature, some based on ethno-astronomy, that would place Lakota peoples in the vicinity of the Black Hills for at least the past millennium.[4] Likewise, Feraca continues the unsubstantiated and impossible to substantiate notions of the late adoption of the Sun Dance from other Plains Indian nations sometime after the supposed move from Minnesota.

While these are inferential historical assertions and have little import for an anthropological description of contemporary Lakota religious traditions, the canons of critical analysis demand, at the very least, that they be persuasively argued and warranted if they are to be mentioned at all. This Feraca does not do, in spite of devoting a relatively large amount of print to this sub-

ject. That other contemporary non-Indian professional (etic) signifiers of
Lakotas and other Indian peoples also have failed the critical analytical task in
this regard cannot absolve Feraca. The academy has critical standards. It
demands proof and analytical argumentation—unless one is writing about
Indians.

Somewhat more useful information can be gleaned from the next six chapters, the heart of this very short monograph, as Feraca attempts to describe
some of the specifics associated with particular Lakota ceremonial traditions.
Chapters 2, 3, and 4 discuss "The Sun Dance," "The Vision Quest," and
"Yuwipi," respectively. These discussions include information that can be
quite useful, up to a point. Yet, even here, useful information is interspersed
with comments and inferences that are misleading, unclear, misinterpreted,
gratuitously insulting to Lakotas, or just plain wrong. The strength of these
chapters, if it can be so considered, consists in the extent to which Feraca's
descriptions can help modern Lakotas verify small bits of knowledge that are
still being passed down orally within the culture and in the extent to which we
can see clearly the similarities between ceremonial structures he observed in
the 1950s and what is happening today. To do this, however, requires that one
be already considerably knowledgeable about the traditions and read the book
as an emic Indian insider. It also requires that the reader (especially the
Lakota reader) be able to "read between the lines" of Feraca's text, because he
often reports more than he intends or himself recognizes.

On the other hand, these chapters contain considerable misinformation
and misinterpretation or interpretations predicated on interviewing far too few
"informants." For instance, Feraca has considerably strengthened his original
suggestion that Lakotas themselves consider the Sun Dance to be christian.
"Many Lakotas consider the Sun Dance as thoroughly christian in origin"
(17). This is, of course, thoroughly wrongheaded, especially for someone who
claims to have done extended field research in 1996. A much more sophisticated argument could be made—by the astute emic interpreter—that an overlay of christian notions has affected the interpretive structures of the
contemporary Sun Dance, but that is an entirely different argument.

In another glaring example of misinformation, Feraca claims that the
Lakota Sun Dance is limited to two days: "As in the old times, no contemporary Lakota Sun Dances last more than two days" (13). This sentence has been
reshaped for the new edition, so it is not merely a hangover from the earlier
edition. Feraca explicitly intends to assert veracity for this claim. It is patently
false. I know of only one scheduled two-day or less than four-day Sun Dance
in any contemporary Lakota reservation or off-reservation context of the several dozen Lakota Sun Dances each summer, the exception being the occa-

sional dance that is cut short for some wholly extraneous and unscheduled reason. The one scheduled exception is a one-time occasion and has to do with the particularities of the vision that has generated this dance.

In an entirely new paragraph, Feraca shows again his greater respect for White scholarship *about* Indians than for Indian people's self-interpretation, as he continues to parrot notions about Lakota individualism (9). Lakotas, like other Indian national communities, are deeply communitarian by nature, and all expressions of individualism occur within this firm communitarian commitment. Likewise, Feraca typically caricaturizes the Sun Dance rigor as "torture" or "self torture," certainly a deprecatory term, rather than using the self-signified theological terminology of "sacrifice" (e.g., 10, 18, 19). The continuing problem with these chapters is that the casual reader of the text could not possibly distinguish between useful information and that which is either wholly wrong or badly misinterpreted.

Chapter 5 ("Other Ceremonies and Practices") is also less helpful. At best, the descriptions are too abbreviated and too generalized to advance any real understanding. Other discussions here are simply wrong. For instance, Feraca's single-page description of what he calls Lakota "clowns" (*heyoka*) demonstrates a serious lack of understanding of the function of the *heyoka* in Lakota culture. His one-page discussion of the "Buffalo-Calf Pipe" raises more questions than he answers. True, he has managed to remove some confusing material from his earlier version, in this case by merely shortening the section to such an extent that it gives very little information at all. The strange version of the White Buffalo Calf Woman story that he reported in the earlier version is now replaced by one that is more common among the Lakota peoples.

Yet even in this sketchy, abbreviated report, Feraca manages to offend. After pooh-poohing a variety of presumed Lakota explanations, Feraca announces with appropriate gravity his authoritative contention that this most sacred artifact of the Lakota people is made of catlinite. Yet he gives no warrant whatsoever for his definitive pronouncement. Again, the lack of critical and analytical argumentation is glaring throughout. All this is quite aside from what import such a critical decision might have on an interpretation of Lakota religion or on an interpretation of the pipe itself in such a brief volume. Thus, instead of discussing the deep and significant meaning of this particular pipe for Lakota peoples and their religious practices, he chooses to continue the etic game of second-guessing something that is not known to any ordinary Lakotas but is preserved, according to Sebastian (Bronco) Lebeau (Cheyenne River Lakota) and many other knowledgeable Lakotas, as a part of the mystery of the Buffalo Calf Pipe.[5] On those occasions when the Buffalo Calf Pipe is brought out for public ceremony, it is always displayed as a sacred bundle, that is, completely wrapped. Thus, no Lakotas other than the "keeper" have seen the pipe itself. Consequently, what the pipe is made of is not important in the final analysis— except to etic interpreters. What is of first importance to Lakotas is that it exists. Even more important, for Lakotas, is the meaning of *canupa*, the pipe that is inherently rooted in this first pipe, an interpretive issue that Feraca avoids entirely. Yet the pipe, beginning with the Buffalo Calf Pipe, is foundational for all Lakota religious practice today. Without an adequate interpretation of the place of the pipe in their culture, his entire discussion of Lakota religious practice stands as fallacious ethnography.

It should be noted in this context that a great variety of euro-american writers have wrestled with or made claims about the composition of this sacred artifact of the Lakota people. There are, for instance, writers who claim to have done what Lakotas themselves have not—i.e., to have actually seen the pipe. They have even gone so far as to describe the pipe in great detail, as in the case of the mid-1960s graduate student from the University of South Dakota who even claimed to have drawn a picture. Feraca's problem is that each of these detailed descriptions is quite different from the others. The pipe is stone. Or bone. It is T-shaped or has a buffalo carved on it. The stem is short or so long that it is a two-piece stem. Yet Feraca knows. The White expert must always know—and must always know more than the lesser beings who are being observed. The truth is that nobody knows, except the "keeper" of the pipe.

Chapters 6 and 7, "Peyotism" and "Herbalism," are very brief descriptions of these phenomena and are fairly adequate sketches, as far as they go. Especially in the chapter on herbalism, one would expect a much more sophisticated understanding on Feraca's part. It is well known, for instance, yet unreferenced by him, that dozens of American Indian herbal medicines continue to be listed in modern pharmacopoeia and that modern pharmaceutical firms have been scrambling to steal indigenous community herbal knowledge in order to synthesize the active ingredients for modern prescription medications at enormous financial gain to the firms. Perhaps these herbal remedies are not merely superstition and magic. Natural medicines known to the Lakotas and other native peoples in North America include the increasingly popular Saint-John's-wort and the preventative called echinacea. Modern non-Indian herbalists prize these and other Indian medicines today as a new find in natural medications.

His aside that "the germ theory . . . is virtually unknown to many Lakotas" is another unnecessary insult, although many Indians today still wonder if the Indian Health Service (a White U.S. government agency) is up-to-date on this theory. To the contrary, Indian (and Lakota) traditional understandings of disease and healing are very sophisticated and complex. Several medicinal plants (for example, the root known as *bear root*) that have long been used by the Lakotas and many other tribes are now known to have antimicrobial properties. While the language of the germ theory may not have been the common category of discourse among Lakotas or other Indians, they did know how to treat diseases that were common in their precolonial communities, and they understood very well the healing properties of native antimicrobial and antiseptic medicines and how and when to use them.

It might also be noted that White appropriation of Indian medicines has become a serious problem in Lakota territories such as the Black Hills as White herbalists rush to harvest herbs and plants illegally in the national forest. A White man was arrested last summer with 1,800 echinacea plants. It takes twenty years for one of these plants to grow to useful harvesting maturity. Moreover, Whites typically use only a small portion of the plant—the root. Indian peoples know how to and consistently do use the entire plant. By clear-cutting these natural remedies, White herbalists are assuring that there will be none for the next generation.

Feraca's concluding chapter, like the whole of the book, is so brief as to be unhelpful. Again, in spite of its brevity, it contains much false information. "All Lakotas think of themselves as at least nominally Christian" (81). This may have been somewhat more the case in 1963 but is most certainly false in 1996, as Lakotas in increasing numbers opt to live solely in connection with the ancestral ceremonial traditions. Feraca's visit to the reservation in 1996 must have been very short indeed, or he would certainly have discovered this growing shift away from the churches.

"*Ate Wakan Tanka*" in the first edition is corrected to *Wakan Tanka* in the new edition. *Ate*, meaning "father," is not at all a pervasive Lakota traditional designation for *wakan tanka*, but is a missionary imposition, an attempt to appropriate *wakan tanka* as the Lakota name for the christian God. On the other hand, Feraca continues to say, "No Lakota . . . would equate *Wakinyan* with *Wakan Tanka*" (81). This most certainly misunderstands the Lakota theological notion of *wakan tanka* in terms of what Feraca calls "power." Of course the *wakinyan* are *wakan tanka*, just as, for example, *taku skanskan*, *unci maka*, *wi*, and a host of other identifiable entities in the spirit world are *wakan tanka*—which is, of course, not to deny the oneness of *wakan tanka*, which Lakotas also affirm. But this is to introduce far more complexity than Feraca seems capable of understanding.

In general, Feraca is relatively clear that skepticism and incredulity are critical to his objective perspective. Yet the racism inherent in such objectivism also is abundantly clear. Were extra clarification needed, Feraca has laced his

text throughout with gratuitous insults to Lakota people. For instance, in suc-
ceeding pages in chapter 2, he manages to announce his superior White privileged position in relation to his observed species. On page 14, he mentions
souvenir booklets published by some Sun Dance committee (in 1963!) at Pine
Ridge and adds the totally gratuitous comment, "These booklets are notorious
for misspelling and anachronisms." If he were writing on the failures of federal Indian education programs, the comment might have some relevance. In
a supposedly anthropological treatment of Lakota religious practices, it can
only serve the purpose of ensuring the smug superiority of both the writer and
the assumed (White, academic, etic) reader.

One page later, in discussing the tradition (presumably) of having a young
virgin cut down the tree, Feraca adds another gratuitous comment: "I have
heard coarse jokes made by the men in reference to the former practice [sic]
of having a virgin cut the pole [sic]." The comment is completely out of any
context that might give it any useful anthropological meaning and seems only
to serve the purpose of denigrating Lakotas and their traditions. Moreover, his
discussion here is completely off the mark again. Never has there been a tradition that a virgin cut down the Sun Dance tree. Nor was the tradition, as
Feraca concludes, that this person might today be asked to strike the last blow
on the tree. Rather, a young innocent will most often be used to strike the *first*
blow on the tree, something that he acknowledges in a new footnote. Without
correcting the text itself, this confusing argumentation can only be characterized as careless scholarship. Moreover, this ceremonial act has serious theological significance for the Lakota Sun Dance tradition and has to do with the
relationship between the tree and the people, a concept of which Feraca
seems completely ignorant. Finally, Feraca must be corrected that this is certainly not merely a "former practice." It very much continues today and,
according to Lebeau, may even be a fairly modern innovation.

At times, Feraca's interpretive posture makes clear his total lack of understanding of the actual meaning of the Sun Dance for Lakota peoples. Catego-
rizing the Lakota Sun Dance as "ostentation," he insists, "What the old Lakota
Sun Dance lacked in impressive formality it gained in various excesses such as
bloodshed" (p. 13). Moreover, Feraca's material on the Pine Ridge Sun Dance
is quite dated in this new edition. The "tourist" dance at Pine Ridge has not
been performed in decades, having long given way to a great variety of *actual*
Sun Dances each summer in various districts around the reservation, as they
are on most of the Lakota and Dakota reservations in the United States and
Canada.

Like many professional signifiers, Feraca has chosen to use a much more
complex orthography in his revised edition. This further compounds the vol-

ume's lack of usefulness for Lakota speakers—who may have varying abilities in reading Lakota but would certainly not recognize their language in Feraca's orthographic transcriptions. It should be said here that there is a more or less customary orthography commonly in use on Lakota reservations. While it is not precisely phonetic, it is much more so than english. Perhaps Feraca could begin a genuine linguistic reformation by adopting a more precise phonetic orthography for english. But then no english readers would read his book.

Finally, unless the reader knows enough already about Lakota culture and religious traditions, the reader is likely to learn more erroneous information than true and helpful information. Many of the descriptions are so short as to give little information at all. The book is really a pamphlet, merely outlining some basically *illiterate* observations of Lakota peoples, if literacy can be extended here to oral textuality and cultural competency.

One can only wonder why the University of Nebraska Press has chosen to publish this wholly inadequate text—let alone to give it the respect and high profile of a slick hard-cover first run. This question alone raises significant sociological and sociopolitical issues worthy of intellectual analysis with respect to the academy and the place of academic publishing houses. Of course, University of Nebraska Press has a long history of dealing in etic interpretations of Indian peoples and their histories and cultures. Yet this volume is so inadequate and so marginally changed from its 1963 version as to raise new questions about the ultimate intentions of the Press. One must suspect such ingrained cultural illiteracy on the part of the Press and the academy as to conclude that academic racism runs so deep within the academy generally that it clouds all critical judgment. Economic realities also enter into play. Given the expanding popularity of New Age interest in Indian cultures and especially Indian religious traditions, the book will undoubtedly sell. And that is the ultimate racism of this late-colonial world of globalized capital. Thus, cultural illiteracy becomes an excuse for venture capitalism and the propagation of racist caricatures, even in academic publishing.

At the same time, this text must generate questions about the author and the range of possible intentions of the author. The frequency of gratuitous insults throughout the text ought to cause any reader to wonder whether mere academic naïveté has not given way to some underlying malevolence in Feraca's case. Indeed, the insults are so prominent that one would have expected an eminent university press to raise questions about the scholarly identity of the author. That University of Nebraska Press did not—and seems oblivious to Feraca's publishing track record—raises anew those serious sociopolitical concerns about the inherent racism of the press mentioned above.

So who is Feraca? This book is not simply sloppy and inadequate scholarship but is consistent with Feraca's other recent writings. As Vine Deloria Jr. argues, Feraca fits into that emerging category of White backlash writing.[6] This is evident in a brief survey of other recent Feraca writings. A Feraca essay was included, for example, in Clifton's *The Invented Indian*, an edited collection of essays that are patently anti-Indian or at least very deprecatory of contemporary scholarship and writing about Indians done by Indians themselves.[7] Feraca's essay in the collection is a transparently self-serving critique of the Bureau of Indian Affairs. As a former career employee of this government bureaucracy, who seems to have bailed out when his advancement opportunities were limited by the emergence of the Indian preference hiring policy in the early 1970s, he writes to object to the "reverse racism" of this Indian preference policy. The running of Indian affairs, evidently, ought to be left to competent White men who have developed the academic expertise to know about Indians in ways that Indians are incapable of knowing about themselves. To make absolutely clear his anti-Indian posture, Feraca published a book that same year with the University Press of America in which he again attacks any Indian move toward self-definition, legal or political activism, and, especially, aboriginal tribal land claims.[8]

In his review essay of Clifton's edited collection, *The Invented Indian*, Deloria includes Feraca in his critique of the assembled authors as "second rate scholars on a holy mission of stopping the barbarian hordes (Indians) at the gates before they overwhelm the old citadels of comfortable fiction."[9] At least in Feraca's case, *Wakinyan* would amply demonstrate that Deloria's critique may have been overly generous. And the University of Nebraska Press now goes on record as a major defender of those old citadels of academic racism. Even with the radical transparency of Feraca's public profile on American Indian issues, Nebraska decided that *Wakinyan* merited republication after thirty-six years of well-deserved obscurity.

7

Indian Culture and Interpreting the Christian Bible

An American Indian reading of the christian Bible presents an interesting challenge to the predominant, Eurocentric tradition of biblical scholarship. Western biblical scholarship has long struggled with the task of accurately and adequately translating a text from one language to another. Since languages are never simply codes for one another, there are always things one can say clearly in one language that may not be possible to say simply and easily at all in another language. More recently, scholars have begun to understand that their task also includes the greater difficulty of translating from one culture into another culture. It was the lack of this understanding that necessarily caused christian missionaries, often with the best of intentions, to function so genocidally with respect to Indian cultures.[1] Today we are beginning to gain some clarity about the cultural otherness of biblical text for modern readers and, more importantly, the cultural otherness of exegesis and interpretation.

An American Indian reading of the christian Bible will differ from usual euro-american interpretations on at least three counts. First, the distinct and fundamental differences extant in a juxtaposition of western christian and American Indian cultural contexts indicate that the prevailing theological function of the hebrew scriptures must also be different. Second, the sociopolitical context of American Indian peoples will characteristically generate a reading of the text that is particularly Indian. And third, the discrete cultural particularities of cognitive structures among American Indians will necessarily generate "normatively divergent" readings of scripture.[2]

The Imposition of a Foreign History

There is, of course, an initial theological issue with respect to the role of hebrew scriptures in an American Indian context. Many Indian christian congregations will give considerable prominence to the hebrew scriptures, because the nature of their narrative is far more compatible with Indian narrative traditions than, for instance, the discursive style of New Testament epistolary literature. At the same time, because of the surviving narrative traditions of many Native American communities, there is a theological problem inherent in any attempt to accord the same status to hebrew scripture that it receives in euro-american church communities.

Every tribal community in North America had a healthy and responsible relationship with the Sacred Other long before it knew of, or confessed, the gospel of Jesus Christ. Indeed, by virtue of the common history and shared cultural identity of the members of each Indian community, the religious controversy that is so prevalent in euro-american culture is conspicuously absent from Indian spiritual tradition and practice. This shared history and identity acquire a singular significance when it is understood that they are *both cause and effect* of a cosmology that does not recognize the world as a composite of mutually exclusive categories that are generally referred to as the religious, political, economic, and social aspects of life.[3] They had a relationship with the Sacred Other, as Creator or Creational Force or Energy, that was solidified in the stories they told around the campfires and especially in their ceremonies. Many Native American christians today have claimed their own histories, cultural traditions, narratives, and traditional ceremonies as the appropriate traditional covenant (christian Old Testament) for their communities.

The imposition of the hebrew Bible on Native American christians as an old testament has two primary effects that are dysfunctional for Native American communities. First, it abrogates (explicitly or implicitly) the validity of Native American traditions. Second, it inherently prescribes replacing one's own history with someone else's history as an ineluctable prerequisite for conversion.

Sociopolitical Context
and a Native American Hermeneutic

The sociopolitical context constructed around imperialism in Europe generated a colonial conquest interpretation of the Exodus account. Such an interpretation provided inspiration to John Winthrop and the seventeenth-century

"Puritan" english invaders and conquerors of New England, who consistently saw themselves as a new Israel settling in a new promised land.[4] Nineteenth-century german imperialism, coupled with the prominence of german exegetical research and a burgeoning *colonial library*[5] of alleged scientific facts defining and supporting theories of social evolution, which endured late into the twentieth century, gave rise to conquest exegesis well into the twentieth century in all euro-american scholarship. More recently, Gottwald and others, under the influence of marxist socialism, have argued for a "peasant revolt" paradigm for interpreting the same event.[6] Both interpretations present a significant problematic for Native American readers.

As Warrior has demonstrated, the israelite conquest has little historical affinity with the American Indian experience. To the contrary, the closest analogy to Indian history in the hebrew scriptures seems to be the experience of the Canaanites, who were dispossessed of their land and annihilated by a foreign invader. It should be readily apparent why Indian eyes would see this narrative quite differently from even Black church folk in North America. As the story is told in the book called Exodus, the liberation of Israel is inexorably linked with the invasion, conquest, and destruction of the Canaanites, the aboriginal owners of the land. For similar reasons, the peasant revolt model lacks any affinity with Native American experience.[7] The class analysis engaged by Gottwald requires the imposition of yet another category of cognition that is foreign to Indian peoples. Native American traditional cultures knew nothing of such class distinctions that resulted historically in Europe in a classification of certain peoples as peasants.[8] While the revolt paradigm may have some superficial appeal because of the more egalitarian nature of Indian communities, the marxist inclination to overlook or deny cultural distinctions in favor of imposing classless social homogenization is antithetical to American Indian social cognition.[9]

Native American Culture and Cognitive Structures

The third difference in an Indian reading of the Bible has to do with more fundamental differences in the structures of cognition between culturally discrete communities. Even when scholars more fully understand the task of translating languages and cultures, they must knowingly take the risk of mistranslating. The risk is not necessarily that they may have failed to understand the other culture or language, but that they are not fully aware of their own fundamental cultural presuppositions. These presuppositions are the foundational metaphors of existence which become formative for thought processes and out of which evolve the discursive category system of every discrete cultural community.

The distinction between temporal and spatial as foundational cognitive categories provides us with a compelling example that illustrates the incommensurability between American Indian and euro-western or euro-american thought. Further, the application of the spatial as an Indian hermeneutical principle can clarify a particularly creational interpretation of the *basileia tou theou* (usual english translation: kingdom of God).

Spatiality and Creation as Hermeneutical Principles

The spatial orientation of American Indian peoples, and their spiritual and political attachment to place and land, is well noted in the literature.[10] As a corollary to this spatial orientation, Indian religious thought seems invariably to begin with some sense of creation and createdness in a particular location. Likewise, the most successful appropriations of christianity and the Bible by Indians interpret both from a referential perspective on creation.

In an American Indian context, creation is not just God's initiatory (temporally primordial) act; it is an ongoing eschatological act (with spatial particularity). Thus, even an Indian christian hermeneutic must press toward seeing creation as the eschatological basis even for the Christ event. If this seems difficult to grasp, indeed, it is likely so because the western cultures in which the gospel has traditionally come to find its home are so fundamentally oriented toward temporality and so disoriented from any foundational sense of spatiality. As a result, all of the categories of analytical discourse in the western intellectual tradition function out of a temporal base, thereby ordering euro-americans' understanding of all reality.[11] This pervasive temporal disposition characterizes euro-american theologies generally, but especially the interpretation of key biblical themes and texts.

That all American Indian spiritual insights and hence Indian theology must begin with creation is reflected already in the basic liturgical posture of Indians in many North American tribes. Prayers are most often said with the community assembled into some form of circle—a key symbol for self-understanding in these tribes because it represents the whole of the universe and our place and role within it. All see themselves as coequal participants in the circle, standing neither above nor below anything else in creation. Jackie Yellow Tail, a Crow woman, offers her critique of christianity in these words:

Life is a circle, the world is a circle. The Christian way of seeing the
world is that within this circle there's a man called Jesus; on the outside
is the trees, the rocks, the animals; all around the world are the different things that are on Mother Earth. In the center is man above all
things.[12]

American Indians do not share this sense of anthropocentrism. There is little
sense of hierarchy in this cultural context, even of species, because the circle
has no beginning nor ending. Hence all the "createds" (that is, all the two-
leggeds, four-leggeds, wingeds, and living-moving ones) participate together,
each in their own way, to preserve the wholeness of the circle.[13] It is also
important to note that the formation of the circle is itself prayer, a prayer for
the harmony and balance of creation; indeed, in some ceremonies no words
need be spoken.

The Lakota people, one of hundreds of distinct Native American peoples in
North America, have a short prayer phrase which they use in all their prayers
that captures the cultural and spiritual sentiment of all American Indians and
aptly illustrates the Indian sense of the centrality of creation. The phrase,
mitakuye ouyasin, functions somewhat like the word *amen* in european and
American christianity. As such, it is used to end every prayer and actually is in
itself a whole prayer, often being the only phrase spoken. The usual translation
offered is: "For all my relations." Yet, like most Indian symbols, *mitakuye
ouyasin* is polyvalent in its meaning. Certainly, one is praying for one's close
kin, aunts, cousins, children, grandparents, etc., but "relations" can be understood as fellow tribal members or even all Indian people. At the same time, the
phrase includes all human beings, all two-leggeds as relatives of one another.
And the ever-expanding circle does not stop there. Every American Indian who
prays this prayer knows that her or his relatives necessarily include the four-
leggeds, the wingeds, and all the living-moving ones, including trees, rocks
and mountains, fish and snakes.

Perhaps then, given the full measure of *mitakuye oyasin*, one can begin to
understand the extensive image and scope of the interrelatedness and interde-
pendence symbolized by the circle and the importance of reciprocity and
respect for one another in maintaining the balance and wholeness of the circle. The American Indian concern for starting theology with Creation is a need
to acknowledge the goodness and inherent worth of all of that has been given
life by the Great Mystery. Accordingly, we experience what christians would
define as "evil" or "sin" as disruptions in that delicate balance, disruptions that
negate the intrinsic worth of any of our relatives.[14]

A Native American Interpretation of *Basileia*

A comparison of an American Indian interpretation of the *basileia* (english, kingdom?) with those generally proposed by western biblical scholars provides us with an example of how the Indian hermeneutical principles of creation and spatiality might function.[15] The euro-western scholarly discussion for the last century has been predicated on an intuitive assumption of a fundamental cross-cultural sameness when, in fact, otherness may have been the reality. In particular a Native American reading begins with a primarily spatial understanding of the *basileia* as opposed to a predominantly temporal understanding argued by euro-western biblical scholarship. In the Indian world of spatiality, then, it is natural to read *basileia tou theou* as a creation metaphor.

As it stands in the greek or in literal english translation, the metaphor is radically disjunctive for any American Indian reader or listener quite beyond the inherent sexism of the usual "kingdom" translation, simply because Indian peoples in North America never functioned with political systems that included hegemonic monarchs. Of course, few modern north american hearers (especially Indian North Americans) have any experiential analogues for understanding the political referent for this phrase, and it must be disjunctive for everyone today except as discrete religious language that has taken on symbolic value quite apart from the original (and ordinary, everyday) meaning of the word in first-century Palestine. For American Indian peoples, who come out of communities that are more egalitarian and genuinely democratic and participatory, the metaphor is even more culturally foreign and must be completely recast. The only possible analogue for the notion of *basileia* might be the Bureau of Indian Affairs or the U.S. War Department.

Since the emergence of eschatology as a central aspect of the interpretation of the christian scriptures, that is, the New Testament, particularly as it (eschatology) is germane to the four gospels and is presented in the exegetical work of Johannes Weis and Albert Schweitzer,[16] *basileia tou theou,* until very recently, has been given over completely to temporal interpretations.[17] That is, the only appropriate question to ask about the *basileia* has been WHEN. It is not that scholars did not consider other possibilities. In fact, the question of WHERE has been consistently disallowed. In one terse statement, Norman Perrin recapitulated the normative theological cant of some seventy years of scholarly dialogue in Europe and North America when he wrote in 1967, "[The *basileia*] is not a place or community ruled by God."[18] From Weis and Schweitzer to Perrin and beyond, the question had been, When will the *basileia tou theou* happen? When will it appear? In the course of the dialogue, a wide variety of temporal answers have been argued, each of them generating a new *terminus technicus* with which to label this narrow and seemingly fixed theory. So our discussions and arguments have been contained within the limits established by notions of "realized eschatology," "actualized eschatology," "immanent eschatology" or "future eschatology," each of which addresses merely a different perspective on the WHEN question.

It was Norman Perrin and his student Werner Kelber who in the mid-1970s announced a major shift in interpretation of *basileia*. Kelber first put forth arguments for a consistent spatial understanding of the *basileia* as it is represented in the gospel of Mark, linking its meaning to expanding territorial and geographical developments in that gospel.[19] Perrin decisively articulated the metaphoric nature of *basileia* language, distinguishing between "steno" and "tensive" symbols and identifying *basileia* as the latter. So we now can begin to understand the *basileia tou theou* as a "symbol," which Perrin, as well as Wheelwright, defines as "a relatively stable and repeatable element of perceptual experience, standing for some larger meaning or set of meanings which cannot be given, or not fully given in perceptual experience itself."[20]

It seems obvious enough that spatial categories do not necessarily exclude the temporal, nor vice versa, yet the orientation assumed by the interpreter becomes crucial. As Boring argued, temporality cannot be excised from Mark's proclamation of the *basileia*, yet to assume, as Boring does, that the *basileia* sayings in Mark must be read in terms of an "overwhelming temporal orientation" is surely overstating the case.[21] To the contrary, there exists the possibility of spatial priority in language of the *basileia*, perhaps in Mark particularly. The possibility becomes pronounced in any American Indian reading of the text because the American Indian world is as decidedly spatial in its orientation as the modern western world is temporal. In fact, any Indian reader of Mark or the other two synoptic gospels is bound to think first of all in terms of the question WHERE with regard to *basileia*.[22]

An American Indian spatial interpretation raises the likelihood that all of western biblical scholarship has worked for a century with a transcultural blind spot. Why, after all, would the kingdom of God not be a realm or a place where God rules or a community that God rules? Consider the possibility that on an intuitive, subliminal level there are two very different ways of thinking, of seeing the world, of sorting out reality. Consider that those who think one way, especially if they have developed a system of discourse that has become dominant and highly differentiated categorically, may have no immediate way of acknowledging those who think differently.

The argument is that those two different ways of thinking have to do with time and space, the when and the where of the *basileia* in Mark. Space and time are not necessarily two equal coordinates in human thinking. To the contrary, one is usually primary, and the other secondary for any given culture. We have already asserted that American Indian people tend to think out of a spatial cosmology; in other words, the most fundamental and powerful images, metaphors, and myths have to do primarily with space and places. For the western intellectual tradition, the opposite is demonstrably the case; time is primary, and space is a subordinate category. From notions of progress, to the casual revelation that "time is money," from the sacred hour on Sunday morning and the seven-day cycle of work, play, and spiritual obligation, to the philosophical and scientific inquiry of the West, time always reigns supreme. Indeed, Nesbit describes the valorization of this euro-western means for conceptualizing humankind's existence and future as having found its first purchase in classical greek thought. However, he locates its privileging and reification in St. Augustine's extrapolation of this greek conception when, in *The City of God*, he explains time as "a creation of God and therefore as real as any of God's other creations."[23]

Think what the world might be like if Heidegger had written *Being and Space* rather than *Being and Time*, or, if Hegel had not had at his disposal the temporal categories that generated his philosophy of history in terms of thesis, antithesis, and synthesis. Charles Darwin built on temporal modalities to think through his *Origin of Species* (1859) and *The Descent of Man* (1871), and western theoretical physics developed the same temporal modalities in ways that enabled Albert Einstein to reduce the whole of the physical world to temporal categories. From this perspective in western thought, all of space is rendered a mere function of time. It is no wonder that the *basileia tou theou* is also discussed consistently as a function of time.

Mark and Spatiality

This American Indian hermeneutic of spatiality might be seen as normatively divergent—that is, as an aberrant cultural reading of the *basileia*. Yet the gospel of Mark has other clear indications of giving attention to issues of spatiality. In Mark 10:46–52, Jesus is coming out of Jericho, where a blind beggar, Bartimaeus, cries out to him for help. The important words here have to do with *where* Bartimaeus is sitting and *where* he is to go afterward. He is sitting *para tên hodon*, that is, "beside the roadside," or "by the highway," or "by the way." After he is healed, Bartimaeus is told by Jesus to leave (*hypage*), that is, to return home. Instead, Bartimaeus "follows" Jesus—a discipleship word—*en tê hodô*, "on the way." The word *hodos* is used in both places, yet consistently, in all english translations, there is a tendency to translate this one greek word as if it were two totally different words, thereby losing what may well have been the author's intentional play on the word. To wit, the healing of Bartimaus comes at the end of a thematic section that began in chapter 8 with Jesus' healing of another blind person. In between these two literary parentheses of the healings of these blind persons, we have just been told that the disciples who follow Jesus, even though their eyes appear to be open, are the truly blind. We are also informed that Bartimaus has a greater claim to sight than do these disciples. Bartimaus, who had been sitting "by the way," who had not been following Jesus, now has a more legitimate claim to be following Jesus "on the way." Reading the text from this perspective opens our own space from which at least one question arises: Is it possible that "the way" here is a *terminus technicus*, spelling out or pointing to the spatial bases of Mark's thinking?

Another example that may give credence to a claim for Mark's adherence to place and space as focal points precedes the healing stories, and may actually be a hint of foreshadowing. The word *hodos* occurs also at the beginning of the gospel in the quote from Malachi and may already be a coded word in that context: "Behold I send my messenger before thy face who shall prepare thy way" (1:2). Is this notion of spatiality consistently present all the way through Mark? What would this possibility mean for our present interpretation of the kingdom of God in Mark?

Any American Indian reader would naturally think of *hodos* in these verses as the "red road," the "good way," the "way of life." The red road is a prominent symbol in much of Plains Indian culture and can serve to illustrate my assertion. Two lines inscribed in a circle to form a balanced cross are recognizable as symbolizing the four directions, but they are also the material representation of the four cardinal virtues: bravery, generosity, humility, and honesty or, put another way, Plains Indian ethics.[24] Additionally, the two lines depict the choice each person must make between the good road and the road of difficulties, the path of community wholeness versus the path of individual achievement, the Red Road and the Blue Road. Indian people functioning within their own cultural frame of reference have little choice culturally but to understand the Way in Mark as an ethical, spatial designation.[25]

Basileia as a Spatial Metaphor for Creation

An American Indian spatial reading of the gospels, then, must combine spatiality and creation, resulting in a reading that naturally understands *basileia tou theou* as a creation metaphor imaging ideal harmony and balance. It represents a symbolic value whose parameters might be filled in as follows: (a) The gospels seem to view the divine hegemony as something that is in process. It is drawing near, it is emerging (Mark 1:15). Yet it is also "among us," in our midst (Luke 17). It is something that can be experienced by the faithful here and now, even if only proleptically, while its full emergence is still in the future. (b) The symbolic value captured by the imagery in no small part includes a view of an ideal world. Finally (c) the structural definition of that ideal world is, above all else, relational and spatial.

The imagery of divine rule in the hebrew scriptures is essentially creation imagery. That is, the ideal world symbolically represented in the hebrew image builds on the divine origin of the cosmos as an ideal past and points to an ideal future. To this extent, the ideal world is the real world of creation in an ideal relationship of harmony and balance with the Creator. It is relational first of all because it implies a relationship between the created order of things and its Creator, and secondly because it implies a relationship among all of the things created. As the Creator, *theos* (God, in the christian scriptures) is perforce the rightful ruler of all. Hence, the ideal world to which Jesus points in the gospels is precisely the realization of that proper relationship between the Creator and the created in the real, spatial world of creation.

For an American Indian reader of the creation stories of the Bible, whether human beings were created first of all the mammals or last of all the createds is not nearly as important as affirming the harmony and balance of the created order. While the balance of that order is repeatedly shaken by the human createds, it is still the ideal state of being which we attempt to restore. While the ideal state of balance and harmony can never be achieved for all time, all (meaning *all* of creation) are part of the ongoing process of restoring balance. In his letter to the Romans, Paul says that all of creation groans in travail, that is, in childbirth (Romans 8:22). A christian Indian perspective would naturally assume that Paul sees the Christ-event as an attempt to do exactly what Indian ceremonies do in restoring a world in travail.

In this American Indian interpretation, the *basileia* must be understood as all-inclusive; that is, if it symbolizes the harmony and balance of all creation, then it must include all things created. In an American Indian anthropology that remains consistent with the prayer of *mitakuye oyasin*, the *basileia* must include two-leggeds, four-leggeds, wingeds, and the living-moving ones, since all are created by the Hegemon of all existence. Perforce then, it is inclusive of all human beings, whether all recognize the divine hegemony or not. Those who are considered to be standing outside the kingdom are outside because they have somehow excluded themselves by their lack of recognition of the balance and harmony intended in creation. This state of unawareness is often the result of an individual's attempts to establish her or his *own* hegemony.

While Native Americans know little about either kings or kingdoms, only a spatial response to the question WHERE begins to make any sense at all of the metaphor. Whatever the *basileia* is, it must be a place. Certainly, the verb *engizein* ("the *basileia* has drawn near," in Mark 1:15) allows for and even predicates a primary meaning of spatial nearness, and in Luke 17:20, Jesus instructs the Pharisees that the *basileia* is "in your midst" (*entos humas*), that is, already spatially present.

Removing the euro-american emphasis on temporality, of course, lessens the emphasis on eschatology. In an American Indian reading, the *basileia* necessarily has little, if anything, to do with what happens in the future. Rather, it is concerned with how one images oneself in the present in relationship to the Creator and the rest of creation.

Repentance as a Spatial Notion of Return

In Mark 1:15 the *basileia* is linked with the imperative, *metanoiete* (repent!). We need not discuss at length the nature of the word for "time" in this verse; it is enough to acknowledge the cyclical and seasonal nature of *kairos* over against the more linear concept of *chronos*.[26] In any case, the mention of a time element should not distract us from a spatial, and now creational, understanding. Nor at this point would it prove fruitful to pursue the verb *êggiken* (has drawn near), which has both spatial and temporal connotations.

More important for a Native American reading is a spatial understanding of *metanoiete*. Here, the underlying aramaic (spatial) sense of *shub* as "return" rather than the greek notion of "change of mind" is at stake. Repentance is key to the establishment of divine hegemony because it involves a "return," namely a return to God. Feeling sorry for one's sins is not part of repentance at all, although it may be the initial act of confession. Even Luke, the most linguistically "greek" of the gospel writers, writes in the Acts of the Apostles, repentance does not yet carry a penitential, emotive connotation but instead carries the hebrew sense of return. In Acts 2:37-38, people feel penitential emotion as a result of Peter's sermon and come to him (and the others) to ask what they must do. His response: "Repent and be baptized." Since they already feel sorry for their sins, that is not what Peter requires of them. The hebrew notion of repentance really is calling on God's people to recognize the divine hegemony, to return to God, to return to the ideal relationship between Creator and the created, to live in the spatiality of creation fully cognizant of God's hegemony, of human createdness, and of the interrelatedness of all the createds. In the Native American world, we recognize that interrelatedness as a peer relationship between the two-leggeds and all the others: four-leggeds, wingeds, and living-moving things. That is the real world within which we hope to actualize the ideal world of balance and harmony.

The Indian understanding of creation as sacred, of Grandmother Earth as the source of all life, goes far beyond the concerns articulated by environmental groups such as the Sierra Club or Greenpeace. It embraces far more than concern for harp seals or a couple of ice-bound whales. It embraces all of life from trees and rocks to international relations. And this knowledge informs all of the community's activity, from hunting to dancing and even to writing grant proposals or administering government agencies. It especially concerns itself with the way we all live together. Perforce, it has to do with issues of justice and fairness in the community, and ultimately with peace. If we take seriously the spatiality of *basileia* as a metaphor for creation and the interrelationship of all the createds under Creator's hegemony, then it becomes very difficult to pursue acts of exploitation or oppression of one another.

The *reciprocity of male and female* in both Creator and creation necessitates repentance (return) to relationships of balance. It mandates a model of *basileia* that obviates male-female oppression and the resulting power imbalances. Competition between human communities is replaced with cooperation or at least mutual respect. Even environmental devastation is necessarily impeded under the paradigm of *mitakuye ouyasin*, because mutual respect and cooperation are then seen as extended beyond the foolish nation of two-leggeds to include all the four-legged, winged, and living-moving relatives, even the trees and hills and the earth itself.

These examples begin to articulate an American Indian reading of the christian Bible. That this reading of the *basileia* may be quite disparate from standard euro-american interpretations should signal that in a multicultural, pluralistic world of diversity, there will necessarily be many readings of the Bible. Normative interpretation, the universally valid hermeneutic, seems to be further from reality today than ever. In the following chapter, we can begin to see how this *Indian* hermeneutic might be applied within the larger theological discourse in the world today.

8

Spirituality, Native American Personhood, Sovereignty, and Solidarity
Liberation Theology and Socialism

There are aboriginal peoples, that is, indigenous peoples, in North America today. I treasure this opportunity to share with all of you something of our struggle and of a theology that is emerging out of that struggle. I also hope to challenge all of you to hear the voices of indigenous peoples in this world as those among the most oppressed, both by the powerful nations and by the so-called developing nations.[1]

We are, if you will, a Fourth World,[2] even as we find ourselves at home here in a conference of Third World theologians. As Fourth World peoples, we share with our Third World relatives the hunger, poverty, repression, and oppression that have been the continuing common experience of those over-powered by the expansionism of european adventurers and their missionaries five hundred years ago. What distinguishes Fourth World indigenous peoples from other Third World peoples, however, is the particular repercussions of conquest and genocide as they affected our distinctive indigenous cultures. While the immediately obvious effects of conquest and genocide seem similar for Third and Fourth World peoples—poverty, unemployment, disease, high infant mortality, low adult longevity—there are deeper, more hidden, but no less deadly effects of colonialism that affect Third and Fourth World peoples in dramatically different ways.[3] These effects are especially felt in the indigenous Fourth World spiritual experience, and we see our struggle for liberation within the context of this distinctive spirituality.

This has often been overlooked, until recently, in Third World liberation theology models of social change, which frequently remained inappropriate and ineffective in the struggle of indigenous peoples for their right to self-determination. In fact, the themes of much liberation theology have been derived from the very modes of discourse of the western academy against which indigenous peoples have struggled for centuries. These modes of discourse—whether theological, legal, political, economic, or even the so-called social sciences—have structured colonial, neocolonial, democratic, socialist, and even marxist regimes that, in the name of development, modernization, or even solidarity, have inflicted spiritual genocide on Fourth World peoples.

It is from this perspective that I want to share with you how an indigenous understanding of the spiritual is integral to the salvation of Native American peoples, quite apart from the struggle toward liberation envisioned by many latin american theologians. I would like to begin by drawing both some contrast and some affinity between Third World theology and what might define a Fourth World Native American theology.

Gustavo Gutiérrez,[4] the most renowned thinker on liberation theology, argues four important points:

1. Liberation theology should focus on the nonperson rather than on the nonbeliever.

2. It is a historical project that sees God as revealed in history.

3. It makes a revolutionary socialist choice on behalf of the poor.

4. It emerges out of the praxis of the people.

The emphasis on praxis is perhaps the most enduring and pervasive gift of liberation theology. For reasons I hope to articulate clearly, however, a Native American theology must find the emphasis on the historical unsuitable for us and will begin with a much different understanding of Gutiérrez's category of the nonperson. Moreover, Native American culture and spirituality will imply different political solutions from those currently imposed by any socialist paradigm. I trust that my critique will be received as a collegial attempt at constructive dialogue leading to mutual understanding and solidarity between Third and Fourth World peoples and an advance for the cause of genuine and holistic liberation. And perhaps we may be able to envision a new socialist paradigm that is less rooted in the pervasive modern notion of the nation-state.

Personhood and Genocide

In an early *Concilium* essay, Gutiérrez describes the meaning of his category of the nonperson in language that strongly distinguishes the concern of liberation theology from the rest of modern theology:

> Much contemporary theology seems to start from the challenge of the
> *non-believer.* He questions our *religious world* and faces it with a demand
> for profound purification and renewal. . . . This challenge in a continent
> like Latin America does not come primarily from the man who does not
> believe, but from the *man who is not a man,* who is not recognized as
> such by the existing social order: he is in the ranks of the poor, the
> exploited; he is the man who is systematically and legally despoiled of his
> being as a man, who scarcely knows that he is a man. His challenge is not
> aimed first at our religious world, but at our *economic, social, political
> and cultural world;* therefore it is an appeal for the revolutionary trans-
> formation; of the very bases of a dehumanizing society. . . . What is
> implied in telling this man who is not a man that he is a son of God?[5]

This is a powerful statement naming the alienation of marginalized poor and
oppressed peoples, and states the impetus for a liberative theological response
to people in contexts of systemically imposed suffering. While these words
frame the experience of oppression suffered by indigenous and Third World
peoples alike, they fall short of naming the particularities of indigenous peoples' suffering of nonpersonhood. The very affirmation of Third World "nonpersons" tends to reify what has been in praxis a *dis*affirmation of indigenous
people for more than five hundred years in the Americas. While he avoids the
language of explicit political programs, especially in a later essay,[6] Gutiérrez,
like other Latin American theologians, explicitly and implicitly identifies the
preferential option for the poor with socialist and even implied marxist solutions that analyze the poor in terms of social class structure[7] and overlooks the
crucial point that indigenous peoples experience their very personhood in
terms of their relationship to the land. The argument and the ensuing analysis are powerful and effective to a point. However, reducing the nonperson to
a class of people who share certain universal attributes causes other, sometimes more telling, attributes to become nonfunctional and unimportant in
the minds of those engaged in the analysis.[8]

American Indian peoples resist categorization in terms of class structure.
Instead, we insist on being recognized as "peoples," even nations with a claim
to national sovereignty based on ancient title to our land. Whether we are categorized as "working class" or "the poor," such classification exacerbates the
erosion of each distinct Native group's cultural integrity and national agenda.
As much as capitalist economic structures—including the church (missionaries) and the academy (e.g., anthropologists)—have reduced American Indian
peoples to nonpersonhood, so too the marxist model also fails to recognize our
distinct personhood. Reducing our identity as discrete nations to that of a
generic, feckless socioeconomic class imposes upon us a particular culture of

poverty and an especially disruptive culture of labor.[9] It begs the question as to whether indigenous peoples desire production in the modern economic sense in the first place. To put the means of production into the hands of the poor inevitably induces the poor to be exploiters of indigenous peoples and their natural resources. Finally, it runs the serious risk of violating the very spiritual values that hold an indigenous cultural group together as a people. This criticism is not intended to suggest a blanket rejection of any tools of analysis, marxist or otherwise; rather, it is intended as a constructive critique of the extant normative models, and of the implicit hegemony they exercise in much of our midst in the Third World.

The failure to recognize the distinct personhood of American Indian peoples has a history as long as the history of european colonialism and missionary outreach in the Americas. In particular, the most devastating failure to recognize the personhood of American Indians proved to be that of the church, including Franciscans Junipero Serra[10] and Jeronimo de Mendieta,[11] and the Puritan John Eliot.[12] While colonial armies engaged in direct genocidal destruction of American Indian tribes, the missionaries were, from the beginning, equally culpable in many acts of genocide. However well intentioned the missionaries may have been, there can be little doubt that they were of a piece with the colonial conquest. Less direct than the military, yet nearly always in their company, many missionaries consistently confused the gospel of Jesus Christ with the gospel of european cultural values and social structures. As a result, they engaged in what can only be called the cultural genocide of Indian peoples, all in the service of conquest and the expansion of capitalist economies. Even those missionary "heroes" who are most revered in modern memory, from Las Casas in the south to Eliot in the north, conspired with the political power of the colonial oppressors to deprive Indian peoples of their cultures, destroy native economies, and reduce culturally integrous communities to subservient dependence—all for the sake of the "gospel" and with the best of intentions. Leonardo Boff clearly and briefly details the cultural complicity of the early missionaries in the european conquest of the Americas:

> All missionaries, even the most prophetic, like Pedro de Córdoba (author of *Christian Doctrine for the Instruction and Formation of the Indians, after the Manner of a History*, 1510) and Bartolomé de Las Casas (*The Sole Manner of Drawing All Peoples to the True Religion*, 1537) begin with the presupposition that Christianity is the only true religion: the Indians' religions are not only false, they are the work of Satan. Method alone is open to discussion: whether to use violence and force (the common method, which went hand in hand with colonialism), or a "delicate, soft, and sweet" method (in the words of Las Casas). Either method was

calculated to achieve the same effect: conversion. . . . All persons must be compelled to assimilate this religious order, which is also a cultural one.[13]

It was, after all, Las Casas who invented the *reduction* paradigm for missionary work among Indian peoples as a way of more gently exploiting Indian labor on behalf of the king.

The consistent failure of the missionaries of all denominations who came to evangelize our Native American tribes was precisely that they failed to notice, let alone acknowledge, our personhood. They saw our cultures and our social structures as inadequate and needing to be replaced with what they called a "christian civilization." Even as they argued liberally for the humanity of Indian people, they denied our personhood.

Much of liberation theology and socialist movements in general can promise no better than the continued cultural genocide of indigenous peoples. From an American Indian perspective, the problem with modern liberation theology, as with marxist political movements, is that class analysis gets in the way of recognizing cultural discreteness and even peopleness. Small but culturally integrous communities stand to be swallowed up by the vision of a classless society, an international workers' movement, or a burgeoning majority of Third World urban poor. That, too, is cultural genocide and signifies that we are yet nonpersons, even in the light of the gospel of liberation.

"God" and "History"

In *The Power of the Poor in History,* Gutiérrez begins by expounding on God's revelation and proclamation in history, arguing that God reveals God's self in history.[14] I want to argue that this is not only *not* a self-evident truth, but that a culturally idiosyncratic American Indian theology, rooted in our indigenous spiritual traditions, must begin with an avowal that is both dramatically disparate from and exclusive of Gutiérrez's starting point. Essentially, an American Indian theology must argue out of American Indian spiritual experience and praxis that Creator ("God"?) is revealed in creation, in space or place, and not in time. The nineteenth- and twentieth-century euro-western sense of history as a linear, temporal process means that those who heard the gospel first have maintained and always maintain a critical advantage over those who of us who hear it later and have to rely on those who heard it first to give us a full interpretation. In a historical structure of existence, certain people carry the message and, most importantly, hold all the wisdom. They know it better and know more of it than later converts.[15] For better or worse, this has been our consistent experience with the gospel as it has been preached to us by the missionaries of all the denominations, just as it has been our experience with the political visions proclaimed to us by the revolutionaries.[16]

The problem, from Las Casas to Marx, is the assumption of a hegemonic trajectory through history, which fails to recognize cultural discreteness. Even with the best of intentions, solutions to the suffering of oppressed peoples are proposed as exclusive programs not allowing for a diversity of possibilities. We must never forget that Las Casas, the hero of White liberals during the 1992 Columbian quincentenary, was just as much given over to the conquest of American Indians as were Hernán Cortés and Francisco Pizarro. He only hoped to do it more gently and less violently. He accomplished much of his goal in his creation of the so-called reduction missionary system, used so effectively—and destructively—by later generations of european Jesuits, Franciscans, and also protestants in both the northern and southern hemispheres. The missionaries of all denominations consistently expressed their historical commitments to the progressive conquest of christianity and what they identified as the culture of christianity—in other words, civilization.

Whatever the conqueror's commitment—to evangelism and conversion or military subjugation and destruction—it was necessary to make the conquest decisive on military, political, economic, social, legal, and religious levels.[17] There can be no room for peoples who consider themselves distinct—economically politically, socially, and culturally—to find their own revolution or liberation. Accordingly, just as the conquest had to be decisive, so too must our revolution be decisive. The Miskito Indians, whose homeland was in Nicaragua during the Sandinista revolution, serve as a prime example of the value placed on an indigenous people unlucky enough to be in the path of a socialist revolution. Summarily relocated from their coastal territories, where they managed self-sustaining local economies, to high-altitude communal coffee plantations, Miskito peoples were forced by the revolutionaries to labor as culturally amorphous workers with no regard to the abject cultural dislocation they had suffered. For centuries they had been a people, but within a few years, they were reduced to a mere class whose humanity and dignity, whose very peopleness could no longer be a factor in the world. The predetermined trajectory of historical dialectic allows no culturally disparate options, at least not cultural options that are decidedly disparate.[18]

Whether in its capitalist or socialist guise, then, history and temporality reign supreme in the euro-western episteme. On the other hand, American Indian spirituality, values, social and political structures, and even ethics are rooted not in some temporal notion of history, but in spatiality. This is perhaps the most dramatic, and largely unnoticed, cultural difference between American Indian thought processes and the western intellectual tradition. The western intellectual tradition is firmly rooted in the priority of temporal metaphors and thought processes, while American Indians inherently think spatially.[19] The question is not whether time or space is missing in one culture or the other, but which metaphoric base functions as the ordinary, and which is subordinate. As noted earlier, American Indians do have a temporal awareness, but it is subordinate to our sense of spatiality, and likewise, the western tradition has a spatial awareness, but that lacks the priority of the temporal. Hence, progress, history, development, evolution, and process become key notions that pervade all academic discourse in the West, from science and economics to philosophy and theology. History becomes the quintessential western intellectual device, and it gives rise to structures of cognition and modes of discourse that pay dutiful homage to temporality.

If marxist thinking and the notion of a historical dialectic were finally proven correct, then American Indian people and all indigenous peoples would surely be doomed. Our cultures and value systems, our spirituality, and even our social structures must soon give way to an emergent socialist construct that would impose a specific and exclusive notion of the good on all people, regardless of ethnicity or culture.

Curiously, or perhaps not, the themes that inform at least some of Gutiérrez's later writing are not the sociopolitical mantras that dominated his earlier works. He continues to advocate for the poor and marginalized, but as an apologist for the church, the Vatican, and the pope.[20]

Culture, Discourse, and Spirituality

All of this has much to do with my focus in this chapter on spirituality. Without an understanding of spatiality as the matrix of American Indian existence, one cannot understand American Indian spiritual traditions. Spatiality and spiritual traditions are the keys to understanding the continuing threat to Indian personhood and the profound specter of cultural genocide (economic, political, intellectual, and religious) that constantly hovers over our heads.

One could argue with American Indian peoples that we must learn to compromise with the "real world," that to pursue our own cultural affectations is to swim upstream against the current of the modern socioeconomic world system. When rightists or capitalists of any shade make this argument, I am clear that they are arguing the self-interest and prerogatives of those who own and therefore control the system and its means of production. When it is a person from a Third or Fourth World community who makes the argument, I am both intrigued and saddened at how readily some of us concede the primacy of western categories of discourse and how easily we give in to self-colonization. How easily we internalize the assumption that western, european, and euro-american philosophical, theological, economic, social, spiritual, and political systems are necessarily definitive of any and all conceivable "real" worlds. We American Indians are just arrogant enough in the midst of our oppression and poverty to think that our perception of the world is at least as adequate, more satisfying, and certainly more egalitarian than anything the West has produced.

As I noted earlier in this chapter, if one hopes to get a sense of the power of our culturally integrated structures of cognition, one must begin with some understanding of American Indian spirituality. All of existence is spiritual for us. Indeed, a rudimentary grasp of the principles of the primacy of the spatial as quintessential to spirituality, and likewise the spiritual as quintessential to not only our existence but the existence of all creation, will serve as a starting point for all American Indian peoples, even though we actually represent a multitude of related cultures, with a great variety of tribal ceremonial structures expressing that sense of spirituality.

Having established the fact that the primary metaphor of existence for American Indians is spatial and not temporal, we have come a long way in explaining what nearly everyone already knows: American Indian spirituality and American Indian existence in general are deeply rooted in the land. This also explains why the history of our conquest and removal from our lands was so physically and psychologically destructive to our tribes. There is, however, a more subtle level to this sense of spatiality and rootedness in the land. It shows up in nearly all aspects of our existence; it is in our ceremonial structures, our symbols, our architecture, and the symbolic parameters of every tribe's universe.

In my own tribe, for instance, the old villages were always laid out in two halves, dividing the peoples into $hu^{n'}ga$ and $tzi\ sho$, an Earth Division and a Sky Division. This reflected the fundamental manifestation (revelation?) of $wako^{n'}da$, the Sacred Mystery, Creator, God(?) to the people. Because $wako^{n'}da$ is an unknowable Mystery, $wako^{n'}da$ had to make itself known to people. It did so as a duality, as $wako^{n'}da$ Above and $wako^{n'}da$ Below ($wako^{n'}da\ mo^{n}shi'ta$ and $wako^{n'}da\ udse'ta$), as Grandfather ($itsi'ko$) and Grandmother ($i'ko$), as Sky and Earth. We should not think here of the oppositional dualism of good and evil that we have learned to identify as typical euro-western christian (that is, eastern!) dualism, or as a fundamental and secular mode of cognition such as binary opposition. American Indian duality is a necessary reciprocity and as such is antithetical to all notions of opposites. They are different manifestations of the *same* $wako^{n'}da$, not of two $wako^{n'}da$, even though they carry specifics in personality just as traditional christian doctrine states of its Trinity. While they are manifestations of the same $wako^{n'}da$, they are different manifestations, both of which are necessary in order to have the balanced understanding of the Otherness that is the Sacred Mystery. Indeed, wako^n'da has manifested itself in a great many other ways, all of which help our people to better understand the Mystery, our world, ourselves and our place in the world.

The architectural geography of Osage spirituality was played out even further in a variety of ways. Most significantly, we were what anthropologists call an exogamous kinship system. That is, persons were required by Osage social mores to marry outside of their own division, meaning that every child—and every person—is both *hu^n'ga* and *tzi sho*, even though she or he belongs structurally to only one division. While this functions politically to give the village group cohesion, it functions on a much deeper spiritual level that still pertains for a great many Indian people today. Namely, each individual recognizes herself or himself as a combination of qualities that reflect both sky and earth, spirit and matter, peace and war, male and female, and we struggle individually and communally to hold those qualities in balance with each other.

The recognition of the necessity and value of exogamous relationships is only one of countless examples of the spatial symbolic paradigm of existence that determines American Indian individuality and community. If one were to name the universal concept in American Indian worldview, undoubtedly that concept would be the circle. Further, if one were to appropriate an epistemological category from euro-western thought—namely, philosophy—one could state that Indian ways of seeing and knowing are informed by their *Circular Philosophy*. As Native scholar Donald L. Fixico (Seminole-Creek) has observed, "A 'circular' approach toward life is inherent in Indian cultures since time immemorial."[21] In Plains Indian existence, the circle is a polyvalent symbol signifying the family, the clan, the tribe, and eventually, all of creation. As a creation symbol, the circle is important because of its genuine egalitarian nature, or what Fixico calls "Natural Democracy."[22] There is no way to make the circle hierarchical. Because the circle has no beginning and no end, all in the circle are of equal value; no relative is valued more than any other. A chief is not valued above the people; two-leggeds are not valued above the animal nations, the birds, the trees, or the rocks.[23] In its form as a medicine wheel, with two intersecting lines inscribed vertically and horizontally across its whole, the circle can symbolize the four directions of the earth and, more importantly, the four manifestations of wako^n'da that come to us from those directions. At the same time, those four directions also symbolize the four cardinal virtues of a tribe, the four sacred colors of ceremonial life, the sacred powers of four animal nations, and the four nations of two-leggeds that walk the earth (Black, Red, Yellow, and White). That is, in our conception of the universe, all human beings walk ideally in egalitarian balance. Moreover, American Indian egalitarian proclivities are worked out in this spatial symbol in ways that go far beyond the purported egalitarian classlessness of socialism. In one of the polyvalent layers of meaning, those four directions hold together in the same egalitarian balance the four nations of two-leggeds, four-leggeds, wingeds, and living-moving things. In this universe, human beings lose their status of primacy and "dominion." Implicitly and explicitly, American Indians are driven by their culture and spirituality to recognize the personhood of all "things" in creation. If temporality and historicity lend themselves implicitly to hierarchical structures because someone with a greater investment of time may know more of the body of temporally codified knowledge, spatiality lends itself to the egalitarian. All have relatively similar access to the immediacy of the spatially present.

This sense of the egalitarian plays itself out in American Indian life precisely where one might expect Indian culture to be challenged, namely, in the ceremonial aspects that correlate to hunting and harvest. The key to understanding hunting and harvest practices is the principle of reciprocity whereby the hunter or harvester engages in some action reciprocal to the act of harvest itself. As is fairly well known, American Indian tribes have practiced extensive hunting ceremonies; many continue these practices still. These ceremonies typically began before the hunters left the village, continued on the hunt itself, reached a climactic point when the animal was killed, and did not conclude until the hunters all underwent purification rites before reentering the village with their hard-earned meat and hides. While these ceremonies include aspects of prayer for a successful hunt, the most crucial theme is that of reciprocity. The hunter must acknowledge that he is participating in a mythic activity originating in mythological stories that teach that human beings were given permission by the animal nations themselves to engage in hunting in order to secure food. The resulting covenant, however, calls on human beings to assume responsibilities over against the perpetration of violence among four-legged relatives. Accordingly, prayers *for* the animals must be offered, as well as prayers *to* the animals in which the hunter asks their immediate permission to be taken for food. Moreover, some reciprocal offering is almost always made: the hunter sprinkles tobacco around the slain animal or deposits corn pollen on its closed eyelids, depending on tribal tradition.

Agricultural harvest calls for similar ceremonial attention and reciprocity. In other words, nothing is taken from the earth without prayer and offering. When the tree is cut down for the Sun Dance, for instance, something must be offered, that is, returned to the spirit world for the life of that tree. The people not only ask the tree's permission, but they also ask for its cooperation and help during the four days of the dance itself. These animals, crops, trees, and medicines are relatives and therefore must be treated with respect if they are to be genuinely efficacious for the people.

As I explained in chapter 6, the Lakota peoples have a short prayer that captures the general cultural and spiritual sentiment of all American Indians: "*mitakuye ouyasin*," they pray, "for all my relatives." In this prayer, "relatives" are understood to include not just tribal members but all two-leggeds, and not just two-leggeds but indeed all the createds of the world: the four-leggeds, the wingeds, the trees and rocks, mountains and rivers, fish and snakes, and all the living-moving things. For this reason, then, in the American Indian world, no animal or tree is harmed without appropriate spiritual reciprocity. Ceremonial acts of reciprocity must be performed in order to maintain the balance and harmony of the world in the midst of perpetrating what is a necessary act of violence. To act without such an awareness and responsibility would introduce imbalance and disharmony into a world in which all are our relatives and command our respect as fellow createds.

This matrix of cultural responses to the world, what we call spirituality, continues to have life today in North America among our various Indian tribes, with the result that a great many Indian people have chosen to leave the religion imposed on them by the euro-americans in favor of a more direct living within and through their traditional ways. Even for those who remain in the church and continue to call themselves christian, these ways continue to be a vital part of all Indian existence. What we call spirituality is for us, as it is for most indigenous peoples, a way of life, not a mere singular category of life called "religion." Indeed, it encompasses the whole of life, and more and more frequently, Indian christians are laying claim to the old traditions as their way of life, and claiming the freedom of the gospel, to honor and practice them as integral to their acculturated expression of christianity. Today there can be no genuine American Indian theology that does not take seriously our indigenous traditions. This means, of course, that an Indian reading of the christian scriptures and our understanding of faithfulness will necessarily represent a radical disjuncture from the theologies and histories of european and american denominations because we will pay attention to our stories and memories instead of focusing on the stories and memories of the colonizer. More to the point, this acculturation to an indigenous theology symbolizes American Indian resistance and struggle today. It reaches beyond the simply symbolic; it gives Life to the people.

Creation, Justice, Peace

With this axiom in mind, I want to suggest that an American Indian theology coupled with an American Indian reading of the gospel might provide the theological imagination to generate a more immediate and attainable vision of a just and peaceful world. What we lack yet today is a creative and powerful theological foundation for the justice we desire. All our churches ostensibly take seriously the scriptural demands for justice, to some extent, yet none of them has provided a persuasive and satisfying means for arguing or achieving the desired results. While Creator revealing itself in history holds out some promise, albeit somewhat vague, for achieving justice and peace at some point in the future, humanity and the rest of creation are bound by the historical/temporal impetus to be in a perpetual attitude of anticipation regarding any full realization of the *basileia* (kingdom?) of God.

As a world of discourse that is primarily spatial, an American Indian christian theology must begin with the Native American traditional praxis of a spirituality rooted in creation. During the late 1980s, I consistently argued in the World Council of Churches that their conciliar process titled "Justice, Peace and the Integrity of Creation" (JPIC) should have been titled "Creation, Justice, Peace." I believe that such a theological prioritizing of creation expands the scope of our possibilities and responsibilities far beyond the existing boundaries of environmental concerns. Rather than the extant and relatively narrow focus on ecology, a theological prioritizing of creation must provide a spiritual and theological foundation for justice. Respect for creation must necessarily result in justice—justice for all creation, as well as justice for all humans—even as genuine justice necessarily will result in peace.

As I pursue this line of inquiry and observation, it will be helpful to recall my discussion in chapter 7 of the potential for alternative interpretations of what I am calling the *basileia tou theou*. I intend to add further insight to my suggestion that an American Indian reading of this heretofore exclusively euro-western and christian concept will abandon the typical euro-western temporal interpretation of this metaphor, and instead build on a spatial understanding that is inextricably rooted in creation. I start with a particular understanding of the *basileia tou theou*, the *basileia* (or kingdom) of God,[24] a concept so central to the preaching of Jesus in the gospels. While euro-cultural scholars have offered consistently temporal interpretations of this metaphor, any American Indian interpretation must, as I have noted several times before, build on a spatial understanding rooted in creation. Western biblical scholars and theologians consistently want to ask the question WHEN of the *basileia*, and disallow outright any query about the WHERE of the *basileia*. While American Indians know little about either kings or kingdoms, only a spatial response to the question WHERE begins to make any sense at all of the metaphor. Whatever the *basileia* is, it must be a place. Certainly, the verb *engizein* allows for and even predicates a primary meaning of spatial nearness, and in Luke 17:20, Jesus instructs the Pharisees that the *basileia* is "in your midst" [*entos humas*], that is, already spatially present.

My own interpretation treats the *basileia* as a metaphor for creation. This metaphor is not used in hebrew scriptures at all; however, the image of God as "king" occurs often, and almost always in contexts that refer to God's act(s) in creation. If the metaphor has to do with the Israelite God's hegemony, where else is God actually to reign, if not in the entirety of the place that God has created? To assume any less is to lapse again into a triumphalist mode that permits human beings, the church, other institutions, and governments to decide who is and who is not privileged and, equally significant, to determine the process by which one might become so privileged.[25]

American Indian spirituality sees as its fundamental goal the achievement of harmony and balance in all of creation. We also see the hegemony of the Mystery (God?) in the whole of existence, but we see ourselves as *participants* in that whole, doing our part to help maintain harmony and balance. Indeed, we see ourselves as merely *a part of* creation and not somehow *apart from* creation, free to use it up at will, which, not coincidently, was a mistake that was and still is epidemic in both the First and Second Worlds and continues to be recklessly imposed on the rest of us in terms of what the euro-american worldview defines as progress and development. While acknowledging that our spirituality is enormously complex in this regard, it must suffice in this context to say that we are pressed by our spirituality to understand the *basileia* as the place that encompasses the entirety of the real world, hence, creation. Thus, no one and nothing can be left out of the *basileia*. In the spirit of the prayer "*mitakuye ouyasin*," we all belong.

Given the holistic nature of the Indian worldview, I must answer two fundamental questions: Will I recognize Creator's hegemony over me and all of creation? And will I live faithfully in relationship to, and with, Creator and creation?

In Mark 1:15, Jesus' first audience is told that because the *basileia* is near, they are to "be repenting and be faithing in the gospel." As euro-western biblical scholars have argued for nearly a century, the hebrew/aramaic word *shub*, "to turn or return," is the underlying notion that Mark has translated as repentance. Then the call to repentance becomes a call to return to a proper relationship with the Creator and with the rest of creation. I understand this call to repentance as a call to be liberated from our human-perceived need to be God, and instead to assume our rightful place in the world as humble two-leggeds in the circle of creation with all the other created.

This understanding of *basileia* and repentance, I want to argue, can become a powerful impetus for justice first of all, and ultimately for peace. What I am arguing is not some value-neutral "creation theology" or some New Age spirituality of feel-good individualism.[26] Rather, it is an ultimate expression of a "theology of community" that must generate consistent interest and praxis in justice and peace. In other words, if I envision myself as a vital part of a community—indeed, as a part of many communities—it becomes much more difficult for me to act in ways that destroy any community.

If we envision ourselves as fellow createds, mere participants in the whole of creation, functioning out of respect for and reciprocity with all of creation, then our relationships with each other as two-leggeds must also be grounded in respect and reciprocity. As fellow createds, acknowledging Creator's hegemony over all, there can no longer be any rationale for exploitation and oppression. The desire for or even the perceived necessity for exerting social, political, economic, or spiritual control over each other must give way to mutual respect, not just for individuals but for culturally integrous indigenous communities.

This understanding of *basileia* would mandate new social and political structures genuinely different from those created by either of the dominant euro-cultural, philosophical-political structures of capitalism or socialism. The competition generated by western, euro-cultural individualism and temporality, and paradigms of history, progress, and development must give way to the communal notion of interrelatedness and reciprocity.

The pervasive nature of the social transformation that would result from such a theology may become apparent in the singular challenge that it represents to the reified status of the "nation-state" ideology of virtually all modern political theories. By what divine right does any immigrant political entity, under the specious guise of a nation-state, assume explicit sovereignty over conquered and colonized indigenous populations? My attention to the metaphysical should not in any way be interpreted as privileging a spiritual awareness over against any physical exigencies: that would obviously be counterintuitive to the American Indian cosmology. Rather, the challenge of indigenous peoples is a socioeconomic and political challenge as much as a spiritual one.

In the wake of the World Council of Churches Justice program, it is important that the theological priority of creation is not simply a priority for environmental concern. Rather, creation is a firm foundation for justice and a

vision for consequent peace. If euro-western christians can begin with an affirmation of God as Creator and themselves as created, then perhaps there is
hope for a spiritual transformation that can bring all of us closer to recognizing the presence of the kingdom in our midst—regardless of political or religious convictions—and that it can be realized now. Then perhaps christians
can acknowledge their humanness in new and more significant ways, understanding that confession precedes return, and that both become the base for
living in harmony and balance with the Creator and all creation. Besides confession of individual humanness, this means confessing the humanness of
churches, the humanness of theologies, and the humanness of the world economic and political order in which we all participate. Given these acknowl-
edgments, it would then be possible to make our repentance, to return, to go
back from whence we came, that is, to go back to the Creator in whom we,
like all of creation, "live and move and have our being" (Acts 17:28). This then
is a truth that extends beyond christianity. In this modern world, all of us must
perpetually return to a proper relationship with the Creator in which we con-
fess our human inclination to put ourselves in the Creator's place. All of us
need the perpetual renewing of our understanding of ourselves and our
human institutions as mere creatures. Our well-being and that of the world
depend on our acknowledgment and acceptance of ourselves as a small part of
creation but integrally related to each part of the created whole.

The American Indian understanding of creation as sacred, of Grandmother,
the earth, as the source of all life, goes far beyond the notion of such western
counter-institutions as the Sierra Club or Greenpeace. It embraces far more
than concern for harp seals or the occasional icebound whale. It embraces all
of life, from the trees and rocks to international relations. This knowledge
informs all of the community's activity, from hunting to dancing and even to
writing grant proposals or administering government agencies. It especially
concerns itself with the way we all live together. Perforce, it has to do with
issues of justice and fairness and ultimately with peace, so that if we believe
we are all relatives in this world, then we must live together differently than
we have. Justice and peace, in this context, emerge almost naturally out of a
self-imaging that sees the self as only a part of the whole, as a part of an ever-
expanding community that begins with family and tribe but finally includes all
human beings and all of creation. All in this world are relatives, and we will
live together out of respect for each other, working toward the good of each
other. Respect for creation must result in an ongoing concern for economic
balance and resistance to economic injustices that leave many poor and
oppressed while their White american or european relatives or even japanese
relatives live in wealth at the expense of these poor and oppressed others.

American Indian people have experienced and continue to experience wholesale oppression as a result of what was arguably a barbaric and uncivilized invasion of indigenous America. On the other hand, we certainly suspect that the oppression we have experienced is intimately linked to how the immigrants pray and how they understand creation and their relationship to creation and Creator. Moreover, we suspect that the greed that motivated the displacement of all indigenous peoples from the lands to which they were spiritually rooted is the same greed that threatens the destruction of the entire planet and the continued oppression of so many people. Whether it is the stories the immigrant europeans tell or the theologies they develop to interpret those stories, something appears wrong to Indian people. But not only do Indians continue to tell the stories, sing the songs, speak the prayers, and perform the ceremonies that root them deeply in Grandmother, the earth, they are actually audacious enough to think that their stories and their ways of revering creation will some day win over the immigrant conquerors and transform them. Optimism and enduring patience seem to run in the lifeblood of American Indian peoples. Such is the indomitable spirit of hope that marks the American Indian struggle of resistance in the midst of a world of pain.

Notes

Preface: In the Spirit of Big Soldier

1. The language of the wa-zha-zha peoples was always a spoken language. It only achieves written status when euro-western missionaries find they have a need to communicate with the wa-zha-zha and especially to translate their sacred text into wa-zha-zha for purposes of imposing their religious ideas on their conquered wards. For this reason, I intentionally and customarily avoid capitalizing wa-zha-zha words, attempting to preserve something of the oral sense of their use and to avoid english customs of capitalization that would invariably bias the reading of the text.

2. Cited from Louis Burns, *A History of the Osage People* (Fallbrook, Calif.: Ciga Press, 1989), 289–90. This quotation is originally from Jedidiah Morse, "A Report to the Secretary of War on Indian Affairs" (Washington, D.C.: U.S. Government Printing Office, 1822), 207. See also Derrick Jensen's 2000 interview with Vine Deloria Jr. at http://www.derrickjensen .org/deloria.html: "That's the best thing any Indian ever said. I teach at the University of Colorado, and so many of my students are convinced that they are free, yet they act just like everyone else. They all do the same things. They all think alike. They're almost like a herd, or clones. They're enslaved to a certain way of life. The thing is, once you've traded away spiritual insight for material comfort, it is extremely difficult ever to get it back. I see these kids hiking in the mountains, trying to commune with nature, but you can't commune with nature just by taking a walk. You have to actually live in it. And these young people have no way of critiquing the society that is enslaving them, because they get outside of it only for the occasional weekend. They may see beautiful vistas and develop an aesthetic appreciation of this other world, but they're not going to get to a metaphysical understanding of who they really are."

3. See Tom Holm's excellent description of Indian warfare in *Strong Hearts, Wounded Souls: Native American Veterans of the Vietnam War* (Austin: University of Texas, 1996). See especially chapter 3, "Native American Warfare and the Warrior's Place in Tribal Societies," 26–65.

4. See especially Francis La Flesche, "The Osage Tribe: The Rite of the Chiefs; Sayings of the Ancient Men," Thirty-Sixth Annual Report of the Bureau of American Ethnography (U.S. Government Printing Office, 1921), 68.

5. Francis La Flesche, *A Dictionary of the Osage Language*, BAE Bulletin 59 (U.S. Government Printing Office, 1932; reprinted by Indian Tribal Series: Phoenix, 1975).

6. Burns, *History*, 290.

I. Liberation and Sustainability:
Prolegomenon to an American Indian Theology

1. Simon Ortiz, *Fight Back: The Land and Its People* (Albuquerque, N.M.: Institute for Native American Development, University of New Mexico Press, 1980).

2. I use the word *community* throughout in a somewhat polyvalent, yet nevertheless technical, sense. For the purposes of this essay, I recommend as a starting point the sense of the term put forth by Herman E. Daly and John B. Cobb Jr., *For the Common Good: Redirecting the Economy Toward Community, the Environment, and a Sustainable Future* (Boston: Beacon, 1989), 168–75.

3. *Promises to Keep: Public Health Policy for American Indians and Alaska Natives in the 21st Century*, edited by Mim Dixon and Yvette Roubideaux (Washington, D.C.: American Public Health Association, 2001), xix–xx, 62–63, 140.

4. For American Indian census data, besides Dixon and Roubideaux, see "2000 Census of Population and Housing Characteristics of American Indians and Alaska Natives by Tribe and Language: 2000 (PHC-5)." This information is accessible at http://www.census.gov /census2000/pubs/phc-5.html. Dated, but still useful, see also Tinker and Loring Bush, "Statistical Games and Cover-ups: Native American Unemployment," in *Racism and the Underclass: State Policy and Discrimination against Minorities*, edited by George Shepherd and David Penna (New York: Greenwood, 1991), 119–44.

5. This is an allusion to Laguna cosmogony. For a literary interpretation of the tradition, see Leslie Silko, *Ceremony* (New York: Viking, 1977), preface and *inter alia*.

6. See Charles Long, *Significations: Signs, Symbols, and Images in the Interpretation of Religion* (Aurora: Davies, 1999), 1–9.

7. See Tinker, *Missionary Conquest: The Gospel and Native American Cultural Genocide* (Minneapolis: Fortress Press, 1993), for a description of how missionaries of all North American churches operated in functional and ideological collusion with the U.S. government and its european predecessors in North America in strategies of colonial occupation, land theft, manifest destiny, and the like.

8. For example, see Charlotte Kasl and Charlotte Davis, *Many Roads, One Journey: Moving beyond the Twelve Steps* (New York: HarperPerennial, 1992).

9. See Christine Clark's discussion of the "construction" of the "secret" of White privilege and how it can be deconstructed by recognizing its three basic characteristics: seeing, choice, and responsibility. "The Secret: White Lies Are Never Little," in *Becoming and Unbecoming White: Owning and Disowning a Racial Identity*, edited by Christine Clark and James O'Donnell (Westport: Bergin and Garvey, 1999). Also, George Lipsitz, *The Possessive Investment in*

Whiteness: How White People Profit from Identity Politics (Philadelphia: Temple University Press, 1998).

10. Analyses of these cases can be found in Ward Churchill, *Struggle for the Land: Native North American Resistance to Genocide, Ecocide, and Colonization* (San Francisco: City Lights, 2002); *The State of Native America*, ed. M. Annette Jaimes ; Glenn Morris, "The Battle for Newe Segobia: The Western Shoshone Land Rights Struggle," in *Critical Issues in Native North America*, vol. 2, ed. Churchill (Copenhagen: International Working Group for Indigenous Affairs, 1990), 86–98; Peter Matthiessen, *In the Spirit of Crazy Horse* (New York: Viking, 1991); Winona LaDuke, *All Our Relations: Native Struggles for Land and Life* (Boston: South End, 1999); and *Defending Mother Earth: Native American Perspectives on Environmental Justice,* ed. Jace Weaver (Maryknoll, N.Y.: Orbis, 1996).

11. Ward Churchill and Winona LaDuke, "Native North America: The Political Economy of Radioactive Colonialism," in *The State of Native America*, 241–66; also, Churchill, "Radioactive Colonization: A Hidden Holocaust in Native North America," in *Struggle for the Land*, 239–91.

12. American Indian scholars have been engaging in an incisive discourse about the legal sovereignty of American Indian and other indigenous peoples. See Glenn Morris, "International Law and Politics: Toward a Right to Self-Determination for Indigenous Peoples," in Jaimes, *State of Native America*, 55–86; David E Wilkins and K. Tsianina Lomawaima, *Uneven Ground: American Indian Sovereignty and Federal Law* (Norman: University of Oklahoma Press, 2001); David E. Wilkins, *American Indian Sovereignty and the U.S. Supreme Court: The Masking of Justice* (Austin: University of Texas Press, 1997); Ward Churchill, *Struggle for the Land*, 37–90; Rebecca L. Robbins, "Self-Determination and Subordination: The Past, Present, and Future of American Indian Governance," in *State of Native America*, 87–121; and Vine Deloria Jr. and Clifford M. Lytle, *The Nations Within: The Past and Future of American Indian Sovereignty* (New York: Pantheon, 1984).

13. World Commission on Environment and Development, "The Brundtland Report (1987): Our Common Future," (Oxford: Oxford University Press, 1987); see online at: www.are.admin.ch/imperia/md/content/are/nachhaltigeentwicklung/brundtland_bericht.pdf.

14. Wesley Granberg-Michaelson, *Redeeming the Creation—The Rio Earth Summit: Challenges for the Churches* (Geneva: WCC, 1992).

15. In another context, I have described the problems attendant on using words like *sovereignty, autonomy,* or *self-determination* to describe American Indian and other indigenous peoples' aspirations. See my "Introduction" to "Indigenous Autonomy and the Next Five Hundred Years," a special double issue of *Global Justice* 3 (1992):

> We chose the word "autonomy" for the title of this issue as an attempt to be somewhat more neutral in our use of language than the word "sovereignty" would normally allow. The use of either word, but especially the use of the word sovereignty, introduces philosophical and historical problems that do not quite capture the American Indian or most any other indigenous context. In either case, it becomes a matter of using the political jargon of a dominating culture to define the reality of a smaller, dominated community which had steadfastly refused to concede domination, conquest, or sovereignty to the larger, invasive entity. (1–3)

16. The United States, through its representatives to the United Nations, has been particularly disdainful of recognizing the status of American Indian peoples in any political/legal
sense that might imply validity to Indian claims on the international stage. For a detailed
treatment of this struggle, see Glenn T. Morris, "Vine Deloria Jr., and the Development of a
Decolonizing Critique of Indigenous Peoples and International Relations," in *Native Voices:
American Indian Identity and Resistance,* Richard A. Grounds, edited by George E. Tinker
and David E. Wilkins (Lawrence: University of Kansas Press, 2003).

17. My distinction between state and nation is crucial. For useful arguments for the
distinction, see Glenn Morris, "International Law and Politics"; Ward Churchill, "Naming
Our Destiny: Towards a Language of Indian Liberation," *Global Justice* 3 (1992): 22–33;
and Bernard Nietchmann, "The Third World War," *Cultural Survival Quarterly* 11 (1987).
It could be added that the first european language about the native inhabitants of the
Americas in the late sixteenth century referred to native peoples as "nations." See, for
instance, the Alexandrian Bull, *Inter cetera,* in Paul Gottschalk, *The Earliest Diplomatic
Documents on America: The Papal Bulls of 1493 and the Treaty of Tordesillas* (1927; New
York: 1978), 21.

18. Patrick Tierney, *Darkness in El Dorado: How Scientists and Journalists Devastated the
Amazon* (New York: Norton, 2000).

19. Michael Hardt and Antonio Negri, *Empire* (Cambridge, Mass.: Harvard University
Press, 2000), offer an important analysis of this shift in the conception of sovereignty at the
beginnings of modernity, starting with the Renaissance and carrying through to the present,
marking the present with another shift in conception.

20. See Morris, "International Law and Politics," 66–67.

21. Ward Churchill, "Perversions of Justice: Examining U.S. Rights to Occupancy in North
America," in *Perversions of Justice: Indigenous Peoples and Angloamerican Law* (San Francisco:
City Lights, 2003), 1–32, presents the clear and persuasive evidence for the consistent illegal-
ity and immorality of the european conquest in North America and the resulting lack of moral
or legal foundation for the establishment of United States sovereignty in general, as well as the
lack of foundation for usurping the sovereignty of anyone else in North America.

22. See Saskia Sassen, *Globalization and Its Discontents: Essays on the New Mobility of
People and Money* (New York: New Press, 1998), 92–97.

23. George Shepherd, "Brief on United Nations World Conference on Human Rights in
Vienna, June 1993," *Global Justice* 4 (1993): 26.

24. World Bank, *World Development Report, 1992: Development and Environment*
(Oxford: Oxford University Press, 1992), 1.

25. See Granberg-Michaelson, *Redeeming the Creation.* Granberg-Michaelson was a
program secretary in the WCC's unit on Justice, Peace and Creation, and moderator of the
WCC staff group that coordinated the WCC's participation in the Earth Summit.

26. Besides the "Brundtland Report," see *Justice, Peace and the Integrity of Creation: Documents from an Ecumenical Process of Commitment,* ed. D. Preman Niles (Geneva: WCC
Publications, 1994.) David G. Hallman, "Report on the World Summit on Sustainable Development," World Council of Churches web-site: http://www.wcc-coe.org/wcc/what/jpc/ wssd-
report.html . The U.S. Presbyterian discussion was initiated by the PCUSA's (Presbyterian
Church USA) Advisory Committee on Social Witness Policy's Task Force on Sustainable

Development, Reformed Faith, and U.S. International Economic Policy, in its working paper titled, "The Sustainability-Development Debate: Where Is God Leading?" (1993).

27. Walter Rodney, *How Europe Underdeveloped Africa* (Washington, D.C.: Howard University Press, 1982).

28. The more rational, economic response on the part of europeans and amer-europeans consistently for these five hundred years has been to argue for the extermination of Native Americans. See Tinker, *Missionary Conquest*, chapter 1.

29. Of course, the most successful economic development venture on several reservations in the United States has been the establishment of gaming resorts, especially in states that disallow or limit gaming and where Indian nations have been able to take advantage of its federal jurisdictional connection that has severely limited any state jurisdiction over reservation territories. In this case, states have applied enormous pressures on the federal government, resulting in increasingly tightened control, and even state control and revenue sharing, over Indian gaming operations.

30. George E. Tinker and Loring Bush, "Native American Unemployment," in *Racism and the Underclass*, 119–44; and Gary Anders, "Theories of Underdevelopment and the American Indian," *Journal of Economic Issues* 14 (1980): 681–701.

31. See Ward Churchill, *Genocide by Any Other Name: American Indian Residential Schools in Context* (San Francisco: City Lights Press, 2004); K. Tsianina Lomawaima, *They Called It Prairie Light: The Story of Chilocco Indian School* (Lincoln: University of Nebraska Press, 1994); and Donald L. Fixico, *The American Indian Mind in a Linear World: American Indian Studies and Traditional Knowledge* (New York: Routledge, 2003), 83–88, 143–44.

32. Leonardo Boff, *New Evangelism: Good News to the Poor* (Maryknoll, N.Y.: Orbis, 1991), 15; and Tinker, *Missionary Conquest*, 7, 131.

33. A very remarkable treatment of "development" as political and economic imperialism can be found in Ankie Hoogvelt, *Globalization and the Postcolonial World: The New Political Economy of Development*, 2nd ed. (Baltimore: Johns Hopkins University Press, 2001).

34. Vandana Shiva, *Biopiracy: The Plunder of Nature and Knowledge* (Boston: South End, 1997), 104.

35. Ibid., 46.

36. Note the insight of Ivan Illich more than thirty years ago in "The Church, Change and Development," in *Ivan Illich* (Chicago: Urban Training Center, Herder and Herder, 1970), 48ff.; also, "Outwitting Developed Nations," in Illich, *Toward a History of Needs* (New York: Pantheon, 1977), 54–67.

37. PCUSA, "The Sustainability-Development Debate: Where Is God Leading?" (2). The paper uses language such as "apocalypse now?" (1) and "historic turning point" (21).

38. Ibid., 3.

39. Jack D. Forbes, *Columbus and Other Cannibals: The Wetiko Disease and the White Man* (New York: Autonomedia, 1978).

40. See the discussions in Renny Golden, et al., *Dangerous Memories: Invasion and Resistance Since 1492* (Chicago: Chicago Religious Task Force on Central America, 1991); and Howard Zinn, *A People's History of the United States* (New York: Harper and Row, 1980). Hardt and Negri, *Empire*, differentiate between the historic "crisis of modernity," of which

the creation of the United States was a significant part, and the contemporary crisis of empire. See part 2, chapter 6.

41. Tinker, "Native Americans and the Land: The End of Living and the Beginning of Survival," *Word and World* 6 (1986): 66–75; "American Indians and the Arts of the Land," *Voices from the Third World, 1990* (New York: Scribners, 1991); and "Spirituality, Native American Personhood, Sovereignty, and Solidarity," *Ecumenical Review* 44 (1992): 312–24.

42. For a thorough analysis of the concept of modern world system, see Immanuel Wallerstein, *The Modern World-System* (New York: Academic Press, 1974); Theda Skocpol, *States and Social Revolutions: A Comparative Analysis of France, Russia, and China* (New York: Cambridge University Press, 1979); and Peter Worsley, "One World or Three? A Critique of the World-System Theory of Immanuel Wallerstein," in *States and Societies*, ed. David Held et al. (New York: New York University, 1983).

43. Many identify the eighteenth century with the emergence of the modern state. See, for example, Cornelia Narari, "The Origins of the Nation-State," in *The Nation State: The Formation of Modern Politics*, ed. Leonard Tivey (New York: St. Martins, 1981), 13–38. It seems more useful and accurate to date the emergence to the sixteenth century with the strong move toward centralization and bureaucratization during the reign of Henry VIII, or even the late fifteenth century with the formation of a "modern" Spanish state in the merging of Castile and Aragon in the marriage of Ferdinand and Isabella. See Robert A.Williams Jr., *American Indians and Western Legal Thought*; and Stephen L. Collins, *From Divine Cosmos to Sovereign State: An Intellectual History of Consciousness and the Idea of Order in Renaissance England* (New York: Oxford University Press, 1989).

44. See R. Vashum, *Indo-Naga Conflict: Problem and Resolution* (New Delhi: Indian Social Institute, 2001).

45. See Glenn Morris, "International Law and Politics;" and Deloria and Lyttle, *The Nations Within: The Past and Future of American Indian Sovereignty*.

46. See *Marxism and Native Americans*, ed. Ward Churchill (Boston: South End, 1983).

47. The Vietnam War was certainly not the first war lost by the United States. That notion is an evil and self-serving lie. See the 1868 Fort Laramie Treaty, which stipulates U.S. concessions to the Lakota Nation in the Powder River War of 1865–68.

48. As profound and self-revealing as the comment is, I failed to note the bibliographical identification at the time I read it and have had no luck in rediscovering the citation since. I suppose I will have to read the tomes of U.S. government documents archived from the period that contain War Department/Indian Affairs correspondence.

49. Daly and Cobb, *The Common Good*, make this point predicated on an historical analysis that compares Reformation theological thinking with the resultant inversion of Reformation insight in enlightenment economic theory (5).

50. Tinker, "Columbus and Coyote: A Comparison of Culture Heroes in Paradox," *Apuntes* 12 (1992): 78–88.

51. A version of this story is included in Richard Erdoes and Alfonso Ortiz, *American Indian Myths and Legends* (New York: Pantheon, 1984), 62–65. See also Walter McClintock, *The Old North Trail: Life, Legends and Religion of the Blackfeet Indians* (Lincoln: University of Nebraska, 1901, repr. 1966).

52. A version of this story is recorded in Erdoes and Ortiz, *American Indian Myths and Legends*, 237–42.

53. See *The Sacred: Ways of Knowledge, Sources of Life*, edited by Peggy V. Beck, Anna Lee Walters, and Nia Francisco, redesigned ed. (Tsaile, Ariz.: Navajo Community College Press, 1992), 158–60.

54. See Francis La Flesche, *The War and Peace Ceremony of the Osage Indians*, Bureau of American Ethnography, Bulletin 101 (Washington, D. C.: U.S. Government Printing Office, 1939).

55. See Erdoes and Ortiz, *American Myths and Legends*. Also see Clara Sue Kidwell, Homer Noley, and George E. "Tink" Tinker, *A Native American Theology* (Maryknoll, N.Y.: Orbis, 2001), 33–44.

56. Leslie Silko's famous novel, *Ceremony* (New York: Viking, 1977), describes precisely such a situation. The whole of the novel deals with the healing and cleansing of a World War II veteran for whom a new ceremony had to be devised. The social and spiritual complexities of disintegration and alienation had made it much more difficult for the Laguna people and for himself. Thus, his healing has to do with the healing of the whole community and not just of himself.

57. For a fine critique of neoclassical economic theory, see Brian Czech, *Shoveling Fuel for a Runaway Train: Errant Economists, Shameful Spenders, and a Plan to Stop Them All* (Berkeley: University of California Press, 2000). Czech is particularly interested in critiquing the notion that the potential for development is limitless.

58. "The Sustainability-Development Debate," 18.

59. For a discussion of indigenous North American alternatives to seeing, learning, and living in a balanced, sustainable manner, see Vine Deloria Jr. and Daniel R. Wildcat, *Power and Place: Indian Education in America* (Golden, Colo.: Fulcrum Resources, 2001). A detailed elucidation of nine specific examples of the imbalance and consequent destruction caused by anthropocentric development is available in Winona LaDuke, *All Our Relations: Native Struggles for Land and Life* (Boston: South End, 1999).

60. Benedict Richard O'Gorman Anderson, *Imagined Communities: Reflections on the Origin and Spread of Nationalism* (London: Verso, 1983, rev. 1991).

61. See Robert A. Williams Jr., *The American Indian in Western Legal Thought*.

62. The smaller, locally autonomous communities I have in mind are more analogous to the communities most affirmed by Herman Daly and John Cobb, *For the Common Good*, 176–89.

63. Daly and Cobb, *For the Common Good*, 5.

64. Ibid., 6.

65. Robert A. Williams, *The American Indian in Western Legal Thought*.

66. Gayatri Chakravorty Spivak, "Cultural Talks in the Hot Peace: Revisiting the 'Global Village,'" in *Cosmopolitics: Thinking and Feeling Beyond the Nation*, ed. Pheng Cheah and Bruce Robbins (Minneapolis: University of Minnesota Press, 1998).

67. See Churchill et al. for detailed comments and discussion of the value of marxist theory for American Indian peoples in *Marxism and Native Americans*, ed. Churchill.

68. Hardt and Negri, *Empire*, 35–37. The authors actually extrapolate the concept they

call "moral intervention" beyond christian missionizing to include what are termed humanitarian nongovernmental organizations such as Amnesty International, Oxfam, and Doctors without Borders. These NGOs are the contemporary versions (in a general way) of the Dominicans and Jesuits at work during the fifteenth to nineteenth centuries as they "strive to identify universal needs and defend human rights" (36).

69. This rather absurd and patently "eurosupremicist" hypothesis is argued, for instance, by George Weurthner, who ultimately reduces precontact Indian peoples to environmental pillagers: "An Ecological View of the Indian," *Earth First!* 7 (1987). For an Indian critique of the position, see Ward Churchill, *Struggle for the Land*, 379–80; and M. Annette Jaimes, "The Stone Age Revisited: an Indigenist Examination of Labor," *New Studies on the Left* 14 (1991).

70. "Sustainability-Development Debate," 5.

71. The reasons for societal changes, especially for prehistoric societies, are still not fully understood. Whatever environmental limitations may have accompanied ancient Maya or Anasazi decline, non-Indian scholars and readers should be very careful in seeing them as precedents for or drawing an analogy with today's *complete, overarching exploitation* of the environment. I would argue that the situations of the ancient Maya and Anasazi were completely different.

72. Kirkpatrick Sale, *The Conquest of Paradise: Christopher Columbus and the Columbian Legacy* (New York: Knopf, 1990), 75–79, 400–402.

73. See Deloria and Wildcat, *Power and Place*; and *Native Voices: American Indian Identity and Resistance*, edited by Richard A. Grounds, George E. Tinker, and David E. Wilkins (Lawrence: University of Kansas Press, 2003).

74. Charlotte Black Elk, personal conversation, May 1987.

75. See Barbara A. Holmes, *Race and the Cosmos: An Invitation to View the World Differently* (Philadelphia: Trinity Press International, 2002).

76. See the revised version in this volume as chapter 7: "Indian Culture and Interpreting the Christian Bible."

2. Indianness and Cultural Alterity

1. This short piece was prepared for an Iliff School of Theology faculty colloquium held in early 2000 in order to provide an appropriate social location for the longer essay, which in this volume is chapter 4.

2. I call this a piece of linguistic americana, since the term is not only distinctly euro-american but has social-psychological roots in the euro-american experience. The term seems to derive from early twentieth century (1910–1915) in the United States. The *Random House Unabridged Dictionary* offers the same ambiguity as did the first of the disputants at supper: "the town or city in which a person lives or was born, or from which a person comes." The radical euro-american nomadism that has so characterized the euro-western presence in North America and the ensuing social structures of capitalism and now globalization,

I believe, gave rise to the necessity of such a category as a means of determining something about one another's social location. It seems as if the first thought North Americans have about each other is that everyone has come from somewhere else. Hence, tell me something about yourself. Where's your hometown?

3. According to 1991 U.S. Census Bureau figures, more than 60 percent of self-identified American Indian/Alaska Natives lived off-reservation, and 58 percent lived in "major metropolitan service areas," which are urban settings with a population that exceeds 50,000. Ralph Forquera, "Challenges in Serving the Growing Population of Urban Indians," in *Promises to Keep: Public Health Policy for American Indians and Alaska Natives in the 21st Century,* edited by Mim Dixon and Yvette Roubideaux (Washington, D.C.: American Public Health Association, 2001), 121–23. See also Ward Churchill, "Like Sand in the Wind: The Making of an American Indian Diaspora in the United States," in *Creating Surplus Populations: The Effect of Military and Corporate Policies on Indigenous Peoples,* ed. Lenora Foerstel (Washington, D.C.: Maisonneuve Press, 1996), 20–21.

4. For a little more explanation, see my entry "Religion," in *The Encyclopedia of North American Indians,* ed. Frederick E. Hoxie (Boston: Houghton Mifflin, 1996), 537–41.

5. It was prepared as a chapter for *Religion and Social Policy,* a collection of essays edited by Paula Nesbitt (Walnut Creek, Calif.: AltaMira, 2001).

3. American Indian Religious Identity and Advanced Colonial Malignancy

1. This rather opaque phrase is an intentional, if ironic, use of postmodernist jargon. It is an allusion to the critical work of Ojibwe literatus Gerald Vizenor, *Manifest Manners: Postindian Warriors of Survivance* (Hanover, N.H.: Wesleyan University Press, 1994).

2. Richard Henry Pratt, "The Advantages of Mingling Indians with Whites," from an extract of the *Official Report of the 19th Annual Conference of Charities and Correction* (1892), 46–59, reprinted in *Americanizing the American Indians: Writings by the "Friends of the Indian," 1880–1900,* ed. Francis Paul Pruccha (Lincoln: University of Nebraska Press, 1973), 260–71. For a brief but informative essay on this project, see Carol Devens, "'If We Get the Girls, We Get the Race': Missionary Education of Native American Girls," in *American Nations: Encounters in Indian Country, 1850 to the Present* (New York: Routledge, 2001), 157–71.

3. Vizenor offers a fascinating reflection on this complexity in *Manifest Manners.*

4. Glenn Morris and Ward Churchill, "Key Indian Laws and Cases," in *State of Native America: Genocide, Colonization, and Resistance,* ed. M. Annette Jaimes, 13–22 (Boston: South End, 1992); Robert A. Williams Jr., *The American Indian and Western Legal Thought: The Discourses of Conquest* (New York: Oxford University Press, 1990); and now especially, David E. Wilkins, *American Indian Sovereignty and the U.S. Supreme Court: The Masking of Justice* (Austin: University of Texas, 1998).

5. See Ward Churchill, *Since Predator Came: Notes on the Struggle for American Indian Liberation* (Littleton, Colo.: Aigis, 1995).

6. Tinker, *Missionary Conquest: The Gospel and Native American Genocide* (Minneapolis: Fortress Press, 1993).

7. See Prucha, *Americanizing the American Indians.*

8. The U.S. Congress passed a series of Termination Acts, pursuant to House concurrent Resolution 108 (1953), terminating U.S. federal recognition of a number of "Tribes." See Donald L. Fixico, *Termination and Relocation: Federal Indian Policy, 1945–1960* (Albuquerque: University of New Mexico Press, 1986).

9. Along with the Termination Act (House Concurrent Resolution 108), the Relocation Act (PL 959, 1956) became a collateral part of the effort to eventually eliminate Indian peoples. The Relocation Act enabled the U.S. government to relocate Indian families from their reservations and ancestral lands into the urban centers of North America with the hope that they would assimilate into the urban mainstream and lose any identification as Indian. See, again, Fixico, *Termination and Relocation.*

10. Women of All Red Nations (WARN), *American Indian Women* (New York: International Indian Treaty Council, 1987); Brint Dillingham, "Indian Women and IHS Sterilization Practices," *American Indian Journal* 3 (1977). Between 1970 and 1975, Indian women of childbearing age were routinely sterilized—without their consent and often without their knowledge—in Indian Health Service clinics. Since IHS is a U.S. government institution, this practice must be seen as U.S. government policy. See Andrea Smith, "Malthusian Orthodoxy and the Myth of ZPG: Population Control as Racism," in *Defending Mother Earth: Native American Perspectives on Environmental Justice,* ed. Jace Weaver, 122–43 (Maryknoll, N.Y.: Orbis, 1996).

11. See, for example, William Stolzman, *The Pipe and Christ,* 4th ed. (Chamberlain, S.D.: Tipi Press, 1992); and Paul B. Steinmetz, *Pipe, Bible, and Peyote among the Oglala Lakota,* rev. ed. (Knoxville: University of Tennessee Press, 1990).

12. Thomas Babington Macaulay already shamelessly noted the colonial need for a colonial comprador elite that might begin to mimic their colonizer betters as "a class of interpreters between us and the millions whom we govern." See his "Minute on Education," in *Sources of Indian Tradition,* vol. 2, ed. William Theodore de Bary (New York: Columbia University Press, 1958), 49. See also the analysis by Homi K. Bhabha in "Of Mimicry and Man: The Ambivalence of Colonial Discourse," in his *The Location of Culture* (New York: Routledge, 1994), 85–92. It should be noted that I and other Indian academics, lawyers, professionals, U.S. government employees, and "tribal" elected officials continue to constitute such a comprador elite today. Strangely enough, it is because we are trained in the discourse of the systems of power that we are the interpreters who today stand between Indian communities and the contemporary colonial powers of governance in this "new" world order of globalization. For an extensive discussion of and by such interpreters, see *Native Voices: American Indian Identity and Resistance,* edited by Richard A. Grounds, George E. Tinker, and David E. Wilkins (Lawrence: University of Kansas Press, 2003).

13. Ngugi wa Thiong'o, *Decolonising the Mind: The Politics of the Language in African Literature* (Portsmouth, N.H.: Heinemann, 1986), 3.

14. Ibid.

15. Charles Long, *Significations: Signs, Symbols, and Images in the Interpretation of Religion* (Minneapolis: Fortress, 1986).

16. It is curious that few sources engage in any historical or political analysis of blood quantum categorization. The most exhaustive analysis of U.S. governmental Indian policy is Francis Paul Prucha, *The Great Father: The United States Government and the American Indians* (Lincoln: University of Nebraska Press, 1995). He certainly mentions blood quantum in the context of early-twentieth-century discussion around the issue of Indian competency (see especially chapter 34, 867–96, inter alia) but gives no real history of the concept or the process of its eventual adoption as policy.

17. Lenore A. Stiffarm and Phil Lane Jr., "The Demography of Native North America: A Question of American Indian Survival," in Jaimes, *State of Native America*, 23–54; M. Annette Jaimes, "Native American and Chicano Autogenocide," in *Indigenous Autonomy and the Next Five Hundred Years*, a quincentenary special edition of *Global Justice*, edited by George E. Tinker, 3, nos. 2 and 3 (1992).

18. Ward Churchill, "The Nullification of Native America?" in *Acts of Rebellion: The Ward Churchill Reader* (New York: Routledge, 2003), 38–39.

19. See Thomas Biolsi, "The Birth of the Reservation: Making the Modern Individual Among the Lakota," in *American Nations: Encounters in Indian Country, 1850 to the Present*, edited by Frederick E. Hoxie, Peter C. Mancall, and James H. Merrell (New York: Routledge, 2001), 111–40.

20. Churchill, "Naming Our Destiny: Towards a Language of Indian Liberation," *Indigenous Autonomy*, ed. Tinker, 22–33.

21. One more example of the destructive psychological and social impact of government programs such as the CDIB designation is reported by Biolsi and concerns the tensions, disrespect, and disputes that have taken place on the Rosebud Reservation, both in the community as a whole and within families. See "The Birth of the Reservation," 128.

22. Community could here be configured as "tribal," clan, band, or family—as long as family is not automatically construed as the european or euro-american notion of family. "Family values" are as important in Indian communities as anywhere among humans, but they will be articulated in a very different fashion than in the broader american mainstream today. To name it as "extended" family is to use language in a way that immediately concedes normativity to the euro-american category of "family." Perhaps it would be more helpful to refer to the euro-american social structure as "restricted family."

23. Vine Deloria Jr., *God Is Red: A Native View of Religion*, 30th anniversary ed., with introductions by Leslie Marmon Silko and George E. Tinker (Golden, Colo.: Fulcrum, 1992). This is, of course, a test of cultural competency. There are far too many Indian persons who do not know their relatives—often through no fault of their own. Adopted out at birth, alienated from their birth communities, raised in an alien culture, they have no hope of demonstrating cultural competency at a performance level.

24. During the past couple of generations, these are the two possibilities argued most coherently for structuring modern political existence: both are universalist systems, presumed suitable for all cultures and societies; both are based on european philosophical structures. While the socialist solutions fit along a spectrum of positions, all modern socialist arguments have some rootedness in Marx and marxist critique. This was true of the arguments of latin american liberation theologians of the past generation even when, for political

purposes, they denied any marxist connection. Today, many of these same theologians have despaired of marxist or socialist solutions and moved toward "civil society" arguments.

25. See Michael Perelman, *The Invention of Capitalism: Classical Political Economy and the Secret History of Primitive Accumulation* (Durham, N.C.: Duke University Press, 2000). Perelman offers a useful accounting of what he terms "the emergence of capitalist social relations" (10). He articulates clearly the historical origins, specific machinations, and subsequent manifestations of the capitalist project, particularly in Britain, giving attention to game laws, anti-vagrancy statutes, and property rights that were enacted in the sixteenth and seventeenth centuries.

26. See Deloria, *God Is Red* and *The Metaphysics of Modern Existence*; and Tinker, "American Indians and the Arts of the Land: Spatial Metaphors and Contemporary Existence," *Voices from the Third World: 1990* (Sri Lanka: EATWOT, 1991), 170–93.

27. If marxist thinking and the notion of a historical dialectic were finally to win the day, then American Indian people and all indigenous peoples would be surely doomed, just as we seem to be under the hegemony of globalized "democratic" capitalism. Our cultures and value systems, our spirituality, and even our social structures must soon give way to an emergent socialist structure that would impose a common notion of the good on all people regardless of ethnicity or culture. See Churchill, "False Promises: An Indigenist Examination of Marxist Theory and Practice," *Acts of Rebellion*, 247–61.

28. Deloria, *God Is Red*; Jace Weaver, *That the People Might Live*; Tinker, "Spirituality, Native American Personhood, Sovereignty and Solidarity," in *Spirituality of the Third World: A Cry for Life*, papers and reflections from the Third General Assembly of the Ecumenical Association of Third World Theologians, January 1992, Nairobi, Kenya, edited by K. C. Abraham and B. Mbuy-Beya (Maryknoll, N.Y.: Orbis, 1994), 119–32.

29. For the similarity of cultural attachment to the particularity of a land base, note the Australian Aboriginal context. See Anne Pattel-Gray (Aboriginal Australian), *Through Aboriginal Eyes: The Cry from the Wilderness* (Geneva: World Council of Churches, 1996); and "One Mob, One Land: Australian Aboriginals Die Fighting for Land Rights," in *Information: Women under Racism and Castism—Global Gathering*, edited by Marilia Schuler (Geneva: World Council of Churches, Programme to Combat Racism, 1994).

30. See the important work of Homi Bhabha and his development of the notion of "hybridity": *The Location of Culture*, 112–16 and 118–20.

31. See Don Talayesva's poignant description of his own educational incarceration in Talayesva, with Leo Simmons, *Sun Chief: The Autobiography of a Hopi Indian* (New Haven, Conn.: Yale University Press, 1942). The colonialist philosophical rationalization for this abusive set of U.S. governmental policies, fully supported or even instigated by the churches, is reported by Francis Paul Prucha, *Americanizing the American Indian*.

32. The Relocation Act (P.L. 959, 1956). See Fixico, *Termination and Relocation*.

33. Joane Nagel, "American Indian Ethnic Renewal: Politics and the Resurgence of Identity," in *American Nations: Encounters in Indian Country*, 336–37. Nagel also notes the nearly fourfold increase in Indian intermarriage over that same thirty-year period.

34. Some of the names of those who have been regularly so accused by Indian communities are quite well known in the non-Indian world of New Age spirituality: e.g., Sun Bear, Harley "Swift Deer" Reagan, and Wallace Black Elk.

35. Morris and Churchill, "Key Indian Laws and Cases," made this claim without much argumentation. Churchill makes the argument much more substantially in "The United States and the Genocide Convention: A Half Century of Obfuscation and Obstruction," in *A Little Matter of Genocide: Holocaust and Denial in the Americas, 1492 to the Present* (San Francisco: City Lights, 1997), 363–98. Robert Davis and Mark Zannis, *The Genocide Machine in Canada: The Pacification of the North* (Montreal: Black Rose, 1973), make the similar case for Canada's hesitancy to ratify the Genocide Convention based on their vulnerability under the convention because of their history of removing Indian children from Indian families.

36. It is beyond the scope of this essay to engage any analysis of the motives for the adoptive parents of Indian children.

37. For examples, see my chapters on John Eliot and Junípero Serra in *Missionary Conquest*.

38. Two relatively diverse collections of essays by Indian authors who discuss "theology," christianity, syncretism, and inculturation are *A Native American Theology*, Clara Sue Kidwell, Homer Noley, and George E. "Tink" Tinker (Maryknoll, N.Y.: Orbis, 2001), and *Native and Christian: Indigenous Voices on Religious Identity in the United States and Canada*, edited by James Treat (New York: Routledge, 1996).

39. E-mail communication. "Bear's" euro-american given name, I am told, is a more prosaic "Cindy Barrett." At least Barrett alliterates with "bear."

4. American Indian Religious Traditions, Colonialism, Resistance, and Liberation: That the People May Live!

1. See Paul Chaat Smith and Robert Allen Warrior, *Like a Hurricane: The Indian Movement from Alcatraz to Wounded Knee* (New York: New Press, 1996).

2. The concept of fetishism as it relates to colonialism and the continued domination of the Other is treated rather well in two works: Anne McClintock, *Imperial Leather: Race, Gender, and Sexuality in the Colonial Contest* (New York: Routledge, 1995), 184–89; and Homi K. Bhabha, "The Other Question: Stereotype, Discrimination, and the Discourse of Colonialism," in *The Location of Culture* (London: Routledge, 1994), 66–84.

3. I argue for the community-centered nature of American Indian ceremonial structures in spite of the persistent attempt of White scholars (the recognized "experts on Indians") to twist Indian cultural values into a more Euro-compatible form of individualism. See, for instance, Clyde Holler, *Black Elk's Religion: The Sun Dance and Lakota Catholicism* (Syracuse, N.Y.: Syracuse University Press, 1995), but also note Dale Stover's insightful critique in his review of Holler's book, "Eurocentrism and Native Americans," *Cross Currents* (1997): 390–97. Stover particularly addresses the tendency of Holler and others to impose an individualist interpretive overlay on the Indian cultures they purport to describe with "old fashioned . . . scholarly objectivity" (Holler, xvi).

4. Perhaps there is a connection here between the Indian sense of *doing* and liberation theology's notion of *praxis*.

5. *National* is used here in reference to the traditional sovereign communities of Indian peoples. It is used in preference to the usual but derogatory words *tribe* and *tribal*. See the essay by Ward Churchill, "Naming Our Destiny: Towards a Language of Indian Liberation," in *Indigenous Autonomy and the Next Five Hundred Years*, ed. George E. Tinker, a double issue of *Global Justice* 3:2/3 (1992).

6. Here, too, possible parallels can be drawn concerning the praxis of liberation theologies and the sacrifices willingly offered by the ceremony participants. However, the preparation and endurance of these individuals must not in any way be conflated with the christian concept of martyrdom.

7. See Andrea Smith, "Walking in Balance: The Spirituality-Liberation Praxis of Native Women," in *Native American Religious Identity: Unforgotten Gods*, edited by Jace Weaver (Maryknoll, N.Y.: Orbis, 1998), 187–90.

8. See Ward Churchill, "Carlos Castaneda: The Greatest Hoax Since Piltdown Man," in *Fantasies of the Master Race: Literature, Cinema and the Colonization of American Indians* (Monroe, Maine: Common Courage Press, 1992), 43–64; and "Spiritual Hucksterism: The Rise of the Plastic Medicine Men," also in *Fantasies of the Master Race*, 215–28. Also see Wendy Rose, "The Great Pretenders: Further Reflections on White Shamanism," *The State of Native America: Genocide, Colonization, and Resistance*, edited by M. Annette Jaimes (Boston: South End, 1992), 403–22.

9. "Ludic" is a piece of postmodern jargon; indeed, it characterizes a particular kind of postmodern discourse and means playful or frivolous. It is the morphemic stem from which the word *ludicrous* is built.

10. See the essay on the "men's movement" by Ward Churchill: "Indians Are Us: Reflections on the 'Men's Movement,'" in *Indians Are Us: Culture and Genocide in Native North America* (Monroe, Maine: Common Courage Press, 1994), 207–77.

11. Andrea Smith, "Walking in Balance," 186–87.

12. Ward Churchill relates a personal experience in which he spoke to an audience in Germany that included a number of what he referred to as "hobbyists" or "cultural transvestites." See *From a Native Son: Selected Essays on Indigenism, 1985–1995* (Cambridge, Mass.: South End Press, 1996), 376–92.

13. Many distinguish between open and closed ceremonies. The Pueblos of New Mexico, for instance, publish a calendar of ceremonies that are open to the public but also maintain their more critical ceremonies as private community events. Likewise, the Mesquakie, also known as the Sac and Fox of Iowa, have maintained an annual program for non-Indians to observe and partake of certain traditional activities on their tribally owned settlement near Tama, Iowa. What makes the Mesquakie's public performances significant is the fact that to this day this small Indian community has the well-deserved reputation of fiercely resisting impositions by and incursions of europeans and euro-americans. They have held tenaciously to their culture and determined early on (1857) that they would not be "relocated" again, so they purchased from the state of Iowa the first of the nearly six thousand acres of land they own and occupy today.

14. Louis F. Burns, *Osage Indian Customs and Myths* (Fallbrook, Calif.: Ciga Press, 1984), 3ff., discusses the qualifications of the *noⁿhoⁿzhiⁿga*, based on the extensive work of Francis La Flesche.

15. See, for example, Neal Salisbury, "Survivors and Pilgrims," in *Manitou and Providence: Indians, Europeans, and the Making of New England, 1500–1643* (New York: Oxford University Press, 1982), 110–40.

16. *Promises to Keep: Public Health Policy for American Indians and Alaska Natives in the 21st Century,* edited by Mim Dixon and Yvette Roubideaux (Washington, D.C.: American Public Health Association, 2001). See also *Contemporary Native American Cultural Issues,* ed. Duane Champagne (Walnut Creek, Calif.: AltaMira, 1999).

17. See Tinker and Loring Bush, "Statistical Games and Cover-ups: Native American Unemployment," in George W. Shepherd Jr. and David Penna, *Racism and the Underclass: State Policy and Discrimination against Minorities* (New York: Greenwood Press, 1991), 119–44.

18. Already noted by Albert Memmi in the context of 1950s Africa in *The Colonizer and the Colonized*, translated by Howard Greenfeld (New York: Orion Press, 1967); further described for the colonial context in India by Ashis Nandy, *The Intimate Enemy: Loss and Recovery of Self under Colonialism* (Oxford: Oxford University Press, 1983).

19. See Ward Churchill, *Struggle for the Land: Indigenous Resistance, Ecocide, and Expropriation in Contemporary North America* (Toronto: Between the Lines, 1992).

20. D. Talayesva, *Sun Chief: The Autobiography of a Hopi*, edited by Leo Simmons (New Haven: Yale University Press, 1942). See a similar ethnographic description for the Osage people: *The Osage and the Invisible World: From the Works of Francis La Flesche*, ed. Garrick A. Bailey (Norman: University of Oklahoma, 1995), 56.

21. For another treatment of this ultimate act of the new imperialism, see Laurie Anne Whitt, "Indigenous Peoples and the Cultural Politics of Knowledge," in *Issues in Native American Cultural Identity,* edited by Michael K. Green (New York: Lang, 1995), 223–72.

22. For a concise articulation of the european proclivity for exoticizing and fetishizing the Other, see V. Y. Mudimbe, *The Invention of Africa: Gnosis, Philosophy, and the Order of Knowledge* (Bloomington: Indiana University Press, 1988), 6–12. Also, see Anne McClintock, *Imperial Leather: Gender, Race, and Sexuality in the Imperial Contest* (New York: Routledge, 1995).

5. Fools and Fools Crow: The Colonialism of Thomas Mails's *Fools Crow: Wisdom and Power*

1. Mails, *Fools Crow: Wisdom and Power* (Tulsa, Okla.: Council Oaks, 1991.) This review essay was published in a slightly different format originally in *American Indian Quarterly* 17 (1993): 393–95.

2. For an incisive take on these issues, see Vine Deloria Jr., "Comfortable Fictions and the Struggle for Turf: An Essay Review of *The Invented Indian: Cultural Fictions and Government Policies*, edited by James A. Clifton, New Brunswick: Transaction, 1990," *American Indian Quarterly* (1992): 397–410; and Ward Churchill, "The New Racism: A Critique of James A. Clifton's *The Invented Indian*," in *Fantasies of the Master Race: Literature, Cinema, and the Col-*

onization of American Indians, 2nd ed. (San Francisco: City Lights, 1998), which focuses on the inherent and deep academic neoconservative racism of the same volume edited by Clifton.

3. Churchill, "Another Dry White Season," *Fantasies of the Master Race*.

4. See Churchill, *Fantasies of the Master Race*.

5. *Fools Crow*.

6. Page 11. Perhaps it should also be noted that Mr. Pete Catches (another Lakota medicine man who was a contemporary of Mr. Fools Crow and a coparticipant with him in the Wounded Knee occupation of 1973) also failed to invite Mr. Fools Crow to visit while Catches entertained his most recent White new age interloper. And he certainly did not invite Fools Crow to bring Mails along with him. What an absurd scenario is described here by Mails. Only the most gullible White audience with a deeply entrenched colonial fantasy for the exotic could find his interpretation even remotely plausible.

7. John Neihardt, Black Elk's autobiographer, conceals these facts from his reader, focusing instead on Black Elk as a traditional "medicine man," a function that he put aside at the time of his christian conversion in 1914. To report his conversion would have, of course, interfered with the White american lust for romanticized memories of the savage, primitive Other that was so decidedly displaced through conquest and persistent colonizer violence. John G. Neihardt, *Black Elk Speaks* (New York: Simon and Schuster, 1972). See also the introduction by Raymond J. DeMallie, *The Sixth Grandfather: Black Elk's Teachings Given to John G. Neihardt*, ed. DeMallie (Lincoln: University of Nebraska Press, 1984), 1–74.

8. Joseph Campbell is a much more sophisticated example of lumping all human cultural experience into a single (in his case, Jungian) framework.

6. Thunderbeings and Anthropologists: A Lakota Primer

1. Vine Deloria Jr., "Comfortable Fictions and the Struggle for Turf: An Essay Review of *The Invented Indian: Cultural Fictions and Government Policies*, edited by James A. Clifton, New Brunswick: Transaction, 1990," *American Indian Quarterly* (1992): 397–410; Ward Churchill, "The New Racism: A Critique of James A. Clifton's *The Invented Indian*," in his *Fantasies of the Master Race: Literature, Cinema, and the Colonization of American Indians* (Monroe, Maine: Common Courage Press, 1992), 163–84; and Elizabeth Cook-Lynn, *Anti-Indianism in Modern America: A Voice from Tatekeya's Earth* (Urbana: University of Illinois Press, 2001).

2. Stephen E. Feraca, *Wakinyan: Lakota Religion in the Twentieth Century* (Lincoln: University of Nebraska, 1998).

3. At least Feraca eschews the argument that the advent of the horse finally made the plains habitable for Indian peoples.

4. See, for example, Ronald Goodman, *Lakota Star Knowledge: Studies in Lakota Stellar Theology* (Mission, S.D.: Sinte Gleska University, 1992).

5. Private discussion with Mr. Lebeau, who is the staff anthropologist for his national community.

6. Deloria, "Comfortable Fictions and the Struggle for Turf."

7. Feraca, "Inside the BIA: Or, 'We're Getting Rid of All These Honkies,'" in *The Invented Indian*, edited by Clifton, 271–90.

8. Feraca, *Why Don't They Give Them Guns? The Great American Indian Myth* (Lanham, Md.: University Press of America, 1990).

9. Deloria, "Comfortable Fictions and the Struggle for Turf," 399. For another incisive emic criticism of the Clifton volume and of Feraca, see Churchill, "The New Racism," 163–84.

7. Indian Culture and Interpreting the Christian Bible

1. George E. Tinker, *Missionary Conquest: The Gospel and Native American Genocide* (Minneapolis: Fortress Press, 1993).

2. The metaphor here is borrowed from Lumbee scholar Robert Williams's legal history of european colonialism of North America, *American Indians and the Western Legal Tradition* (Oxford: Oxford University Press, 1990).

3. Vine Deloria Jr., *God Is Red: A Native View of Religion*, 2nd ed. (Golden, Colo.: Fulcrum, 2003), 100. Further treatment of the absence of controversy in American Indian communities can be found in an essay by Andrea Smith (Cherokee), "Walking in Balance: The Spirituality-Liberation Praxis of Native Women," in *Native American Religious Identity: Unforgotten Gods*, edited by Jace Weaver (Maryknoll, N.Y.: Orbis, 1998). Smith notes that oral tradition and "practice-centered" spirituality allow for much greater flexibility than the orthodoxy of a "belief-centered" religion, which requires the affirmation of certain specific doctrines (181).

4. See Tinker, *Missionary Conquest*, 10; Peter N. Carroll, *Puritanism and the Wilderness: The Intellectual Significance of the New England Frontier, 1629–1700* (New York: Columbia University Press, 1969), 61–72; and Avihu Zakai, *Exile and Kingdom: History and Apocalypse in the Puritan Migration to America* (Cambridge: Cambridge University Press, 1992), 65–72.

5. The scope of this essay precludes any attempt at an exhaustive explanation of the colonial library's composition or the scope of its impact. However, the library's essential—and essentializing—role in european and euro-american projects of colonialism and imperialism is treated at length by a number of scholars. Three scholars of note are V. Y. Mudimbe, *The Invention of Africa: Gnosis, Philosophy, and the Order of Knowledge* (Bloomington: Indiana University Press, 1988); Gaurav Desai, *Subject to Colonialism: African Self-Fashioning and the Colonial Library* (Durham: Duke University Press, 2001); and Linda Tuhiwai Smith, *Decolonizing Methodologies: Research and Indigenous Peoples* (London: Zed Books, 1999).

6. Norman K. Gottwald, *Tribes of Yahweh: A Sociology of the Religion of Liberated Israel*, 1250–1050 B.C.E. (Maryknoll, N.Y.: Orbis, 1979).

7. Robert Warrior, "Canaanites, Cowboys, and Indians: Deliverance, Conquest, and Liberation Theology Today," *Christianity and Crisis* 49 (1989): 261–65. See also the response to Warrior by William E. Baldridge, "Native American Theology: A Biblical Basis," *Christianity and Crisis* 50 (1990): 180–81.

8. See chapters 1 and 8 of this volume, in which I offer detailed explanations regarding the inappropriateness of the marxist model for improving the circumstances and lives of American Indians.

9. Tinker, "Spirituality, Native American Personhood, Sovereignty, and Solidarity," *Ecumenical Review* 44 (1992): 312–24; Glenn T. Morris and Ward Churchill, "Between a Rock and a Hard Place: Left-Wing Revolution, Right-Wing Reaction, and the Destruction of Indigenous People," *Cultural Survival Quarterly* 11 (1987): 17–24.

10. Vine Deloria Jr., *God Is Red: A Native View of Religion,* rev. ed. (Golden, Colo.: Fulcrum, 2003); Deloria, *The Metaphysics of Modern Existence* (New York: Harper and Row, 1979); Ward Churchill, "The Earth Is Our Mother: Struggles for American Indian Land and Liberation in the Contemporary United States," in *The State of Native America,* edited by Annette Jaimes (Boston: South End Press, 1992), 139–88; Tinker, "Native Americans and the Land: The End of Living and the Beginning of Survival," *Word and World* 6 (1986): 66–74; and Tinker, "American Indians and the Arts of the Land: Spatial Metaphors and Contemporary Existence," *Voices from the Third World* 14 (1991), 170–93.

11. So argues Robert A. Nisbet, *Social Change and History: Aspects of the Western Theory of Development* (New York: Oxford University Press: 1969). While Nisbet rightly sees temporality as important for understanding all western culture, he also finds this aspect to be wholly positive. I, of course, find it wholly problematic.

12. Mark St. Pierre and Tilda Long Soldier, *Walking in the Sacred Manner: Healers, Dreamers, and Pipe Carriers—Medicine Women of the Plains Indians* (New York: Simon and Schuster, 1995), 14.

13. It is through the creation stories that the two-leggeds (humans) understand that they constitute the youngest nation of all created nations. Therefore, not only must the two-leggeds live in respectful relationship with the rest of creation, we must learn how by observing and listening to our older relatives.

14. For an in-depth explication of the creation/theology relationship, see *A Native American Theology,* edited by Clara Sue Kidwell, Homer Noley, and George E. Tinker (Maryknoll, N.Y.: Orbis, 2001).

15. For a fuller treatment of this example, see Marie-Therese Archambault and G. Tinker, "A Native American Interpretation of *Basileia Tou Theou,*" in *Text and Experience: Towards a Cultural Exegesis of the Bible,* edited by Daniel Smith Christopher (Sheffield: Sheffield Academic Press, 1995), 299–315.

16. Johannes Weis, *Die Predigt Jesu von Reich Gottes* (1892); Albert Schweitzer, *Das Abendmahl in Zusammenhang mit dem Leben Jesu und der Geschichte des Urchristentums* (Tübingen: Mohr, 1901); and Schweitzer, *Von Reimarus zu Wrede: Eine Geschichte der Leben- Jesu-Forschung* (Tübingen: Mohr, 1906).

17. See *The Kingdom of God in the Teaching of Jesus,* ed. Bruce Chilton (Minneapolis: Fortress Press, 1984); and *The Kingdom of God in 20th Century Interpretation,* ed. Wendell Willis (Peabody, Mass.: Hendrickson, 1987).

18. Norman K. Perrin, *Rediscovering the Teaching of Jesus* (New York: Harper and Row, 1967), 55.

19. Werner Kelber, *The Kingdom in Mark: A New Place and a New Time* (Philadelphia: Fortress Press, 1974).

20. Perrin, *Jesus and the Language of the Kingdom: Symbol and Metaphor in New Testament Interpretation* (Philadelphia: Fortress Press, 1976), 30; and Philip Ellis Wheelwright, *Metaphor and Reality* (Bloomington: Indiana University Press, 1962), 92.

21. M. Eugene Boring, "The Kingdom of God in Mark," in Willis, *The Kingdom of God in 20th Century Interpretation*, 140.

22. Realizing that the metaphor presents problems to modern readers, many scholars have attempted to offer new translations, emphasizing the resulting relationship between believer and God, or emphasizing, as Perrin did originally, the activity of God as King. The most common translation offered is "reign of God," which Bultmann uses throughout his *Theology of the New Testament.*, trans. Kendrick Grobel (New York: Scribner, 1951–1955). On the other hand, the translation "realm of God" is consistently disallowed as an unthinkable translation, because it would introduce spatiality unto the discussion.

23. Nisbet, *History of the Idea of Progress* (New York: Basic, 1980). Nisbet observes that for Augustine, "time was an almost obsessive concept." He was concerned with affirming the primacy of "progress" as defined through "the education of the human race," which necessarily required a context of the "unilinear flow of time," in order to chart humanity's progress (62).

23. Kidwell, Noley, and Tinker, *A Native American Theology*, 47.

24. Although they were firmly committed to an eschatological interpretation as the accepted model in biblical studies in the 1930s, Lohmeyer and Lightfoot were already recognizing geography as an important interpretive issue in the gospels. The use of geography in the enigmatic ending of the gospel becomes another indication of spatiality that might argue for a spatial interpretation of *basileia*. See Ernst Lohmeyer, *Galiläa und Jerusalem* (Göttingen: Vandenhoeck and Ruprecht, 1936); and Robert H. Lightfoot, *Locality and Doctrine in the Gospels* (New York: Harper, 1938).

25. If Mark is indeed talking about cyclical time, we ought to consider the likelihood that he does not have in mind some linear progression of history. This might serve to disabuse western biblical scholars of their so-called "history of salvation," with its midpoint being the birth, life, and death of Jesus. The "history of salvation" has been most explicitly spelled out by Hans Conzelmann in his book about the gospel of Luke, *Die Mitte der Zeit*, loosely translated into english as *The Theology of St. Luke* (New York: Harper, 1960). For a more general treatment, see Oscar Cullmann, *Salvation in History* (New York: Harper, 1967).

8. Spirituality, Native American Personhood, Sovereignty, and Solidarity: Liberation Theology and Socialism

1. The original venue for this chapter was a plenary presentation at the Fourth General Assembly of the Ecumenical Association of Third World Theologians in 1992 in Nairobi, Kenya. The basic format remains essentially unchanged from its original presentation although the essay has been updated and edited for this edition.

2. See *The Fourth World: Victims of Group Oppression, Eight Reports from the Field Work of the Minority Rights Group,* ed. Ben Whitaker (New York: Schocken, 1972).

3. Julian Burger, *Report from the Frontier: The State of the World's Indigenous Peoples* (London: Zed, 1987).

4. It should be noted that Gustavo Gutiérrez is also a native person, indigenous to the land that is today called Peru.

5. "Liberation, Theology, and Proclamation," in *The Mystical and Political Dimension of the Christian Faith*, edited by Claude Geffré and Gustavo Gutiérrez (New York: Herder and Herder, 1974), 69.

6. See Gutiérrez's essay "Theology and the Social Sciences," in *The Truth Shall Make You Free: Confrontations*, trans. Matthew J. O'Connell (Maryknoll, N.Y.: Orbis, 1990).

7. See Gutiérrez, *Praxis de Liberacion y Fe Christiana* (San Antonio: Mexican American Cultural Center, 1974), p. 19; José Míguez Bonino, *Doing Theology in a Revolutionary Situation* (Philadelphia: Fortress Press, 1975), esp. 85–97, 147ff.; Hugo Assmann, *Theology for a Nomad Church*, trans. Paul Burns (Maryknoll, N.Y.: Orbis Books, 1976); and Juan Luis Segundo, *Liberation of Theology*, trans. John Drury (Maryknoll, N.Y.: Orbis Books, 1976), esp. 115. His later denials notwithstanding, it must also be noted that Gutiérrez clearly states, "Attempts to bring about changes within the existing order have proven futile. This analysis of the situation is at the level of scientific rationality. Only a radical change from the status quo, that is, a profound transformation of the private property system, access to power of the exploited class and a social revolution that would break this dependence would allow for the change to a new society, *a socialist society*" [emphasis added]; *A Theology of Liberation* (Maryknoll, N.Y.: Orbis Books, 1973), 26–27. While American Indian commentators might agree with his analysis of the capitalist systemic whole, they would not be so quick to name another eurowestern political philosophy as the solution.

8. Segundo is most explicit in this regard when he argues for the sacrifice of "minority" freedoms for the sake of improving the well-being of the "masses": "Minority aspects (e.g., freedom of thought, freedom of religion, freedom for christian political actions) seem to be systematically overvalued in comparison with factors that are more revolutionary because they affect great human masses at one extreme of the process, e.g. in conditions of dire poverty, ignorance, disease and death" (*Liberation of Theology*, 89). Gutiérrez, in his recitation of dependency theory, argues to expand the analysis beyond that of a confrontation between nations to an analysis of class struggle: "But only a class analysis will enable us to see what is really involved in the opposition between oppressed countries and dominant peoples" (*A Theology of Liberation*, 87). Both levels of his analysis, however, begin with assumptions about the validity of the nation-state. Moreover, class analysis has not yet been developed to analyze or significantly treat small culturally integrous communities, except as part of a larger, more amorphous class grouping. Certainly, to devise strategies for such a level of analysis would require a categorically distinct nomenclature from that used in class analyses.

9. The north american catholic bishops fell into a similar pattern in their epistle on the economy, suggesting the right to have a job as an immediate basic human right. See George E. Tinker, "Does All People Include Native Peoples?" in *God, Goods, and the Common Good*, edited by Charles P. Lutz (Minneapolis: Augsburg Books, 1987).

10. Serra and his missionaries functioned as an arm of the civil government of the viceroy and were remunerated as such while simultaneously "serving" the church. See George E. Tinker, *Missionary Conquest: The Gospel and Native American Genocide* (Minneapolis: Fortress Press, 1993), 43.

11. Mendieta, while ostensibly a protector of the Indians, wrote, "They [Indians] need the whip as much as the bread that they eat," and "They cannot be compared to nor put on

the same level as any peoples known before them, but only to youngsters who have not yet reached maturity." Georges Baudot, "Amerindian Image and Utopian Project," in *Amerindian Images and the Legacy of Columbus*, edited by Rene Jara and Nicholas Spadaccini (Minneapolis: University of Minnesota Press, 1992), 388–89.

12. Eliot used political power to tear asunder the Indians social fabric as well as cause them to become dependent on the invaders. See Tinker, *Missionary Conquest*, 26.

13. *New Evangelization: Good News to the Poor*, trans. Robert R. Barr (Maryknoll, N.Y.: Orbis, 1991), 15. For a more detailed treatment of the "best intentioned" work of missionaries, see Tinker, *Missionary Conquest*.

14. Gutiérrez, *The Power of the Poor in History*, trans. Robert R. Barr (Maryknoll, N.Y.: Orbis, 1983), 5–6.

15. Elizondo, in distinguishing between the "old" churches of the First World and the young churches of the Third World, says of the old churches, "They are encumbered by centuries of traditions of seeing themselves as THE Church and their missionaries carried their model of Church to many parts of the world as if it were the one and only model of the Church. This myopia was simply the product of the interiorized culture of the Church seeing itself through the optic of the empire or the optic of the sociological model of the monarchy." Virgil Elizondo, "Conditions and Criteria for Authentic Inter-Cultural Theological Dialogue," in *Different Theologies, Common Responsibility: Babel or Pentecost?* edited by Claude Geffré, Gustavo Gutiérrez, and V. Elizondo (Edinburgh: T. and T. Clark, 1984), 21.

16. This impetus, no doubt, is the reason the early Gutiérrez felt the need to trace the historical intellectual development of *all humankind* from Kant to Hegel, to Marx, to Freud and finally to Marcuse, completely oblivious to the history of human thought in his native Peru (*A Theology of Liberation*, 30–32).

17. Robert A. Williams Jr., *The American Indian in Western Legal Thought: The Discourses of Conquest* (New York: Oxford University Press, 1990).

18. The effect of the sandinista imposition of class notions on the Miskito people continues in the postsocialist context of Nicaragua.

19. See Vine Deloria Jr., *God Is Red: A Native View of Religion*, 30th anniversary ed. (Golden, Colo.: Fulcrum, 2003); Deloria, *The Metaphysics of Modern Existence* (New York: Harper and Row, 1979); and Tinker, "American Indians and the Arts of the Land: Spatial Metaphors and Contemporary Existence," *Voices from the Third World* 14, no. 2 (December 1991), 170–93.

20. See particularly Gutiérrez, *The Density of the Present: Selected Writings* (Maryknoll, N.Y.: Orbis, 1999).

21. Donald L. Fixico, *The American Indian Mind in a Linear World: American Indian Studies and Traditional Knowledge* (New York: Routledge, 2003), 42. Chapter 3, "American Indian Circular Philosophy," gives an excellent account of the significance of the circle, in both traditional and contemporary Indian thought.

22. Ibid.

23. Wendat scholar Georges E. Sioui states, "For Wendats, the first social principle is recognition of the Great Sacred Circle of Life—the Circle of relationships" and he adds, "Human society must conform to the Circle." *Huron-Wendat: The Heritage of the Circle*, rev. ed., trans. Jane Brierley (Vancouver: UBC Press, 1999), 114.

24. Recall from chapter 7 that I use the greek word *basileia* as a way of avoiding the unnecessarily sexist language of the usual english translation. Of course, the metaphor itself makes little sense to American Indian peoples when it is literally translated. The praxis of our existence allows for no experiential knowledge about kings, queens, or other monarchical rulers—despite all the White settlers who claim descent from a Cherokee princess.

25. I use the word *privilege* here not only in an economic, social, and political sense, but specifically in a soteriological sense. We dare not pretend that these two categories are unrelated in western theology. Certainly they were thoroughly intertwined in the missionary evangelization of Native American peoples.

26. "Creation theology" is, of course, a phrase and a concept widely attributed to Matthew Fox.

Index

Acoma, 1–2, 9

Acts 2:37-38, 27

a-ki'-da ton-ka. See Big Soldier

Adoption, 48–50

Alcoholism, 3, 69

Alexander the Great, 62

Alienation, 3

American Indian Movement (AIM), 53, 56, 61

Anasazi peoples, 24–25

Anderson, Benedict, *Imagined Communities*, 21

Andrews, Lynn, 61
  Medicine Woman, 74

Anthropocentrism, 92

Apache, 6

Approval, White, 69

Aragon, Spain, 21

Aristotle, 62

Assimilation, 46–47

Atrocities, history of, 6

Augustine, Saint, 95, 134 n.23

Australian Aboriginals, 127 n.29

Autonomy, 7, 21

Bartimaus, 95

Basileia, 93–99, 111–13, 137 n.24

Bhabha, Homi, 127 n.30

BIA. *See* Bureau of Indian Affairs

Bible
  cognitive structures in, 90–91
  and Indian culture, 88–99

Big Mountain, Ariz., 6

Big Soldier, ix–xi

Black Elk, Nicholas, 75

Black Elk, Wallace, 127 n.34

Black Hills, So. Dak., Sioux land reclamation, 6

Blackfoot tobacco story, 16–17

Blood quantum, 40–41
  See also Lost-bloods

Blue road, 96

Boff, Leonardo, 103

Bondage. *See* Oppression

Borders, state, 13–14

Boring, Eugene, 94

Brundtland Report (United Nations), 6, 9

Buffalo Calf Pipe, 82–83

Bultmann, Rudolf Karl, 134 n.22

Bureau of Indian Affairs (BIA), 9, 69, 93

Burns, Louis, *A History of the Osage People*, 116 n.2

Calvinism, 22–23

Campbell, Joseph, 131 n.8

Capitalism, basis of, 23

Carlisle Indian School (Penn.), 38